THIS WAY TO THE GRAND AS-IS

New and Selected Poems

AARON ANSTETT

© 1997, 2005, 2007, 2014, 2016, 2017, 2020 by Aaron Anstett

Some of the *New Poems* first appeared in *harlequin creature*, *Phantom Drift*, *Poetry Northwest*, and *Pageboy Magazine*. *Sustenance* was published in full by New Rivers Press; *No Accident* by the Backwaters Press; *Each Place the Body's* by Ghost Road Press; *Insofar as Heretofore* by the Backwaters Press; *Moreover* and *Please State the Nature of Your Emergency* by Sagging Meniscus Press.

All Rights Reserved.

Set in Williams Caslon Text with LaTeX.

ISBN: 978-1-944697-84-6 (paperback)
ISBN: 978-1-944697-85-3 (ebook)
Library of Congress Control Number: 2020933154

Sagging Meniscus Press
Montclair, New Jersey
saggingmeniscus.com

For Lesley

Contents

New Poems	1
From *Sustenance* (1997)	33
From *No Accident* (2005)	65
From *Each Place the Body's* (2007)	101
From *Insofar as Heretofore* (2014)	127
From *Moreover* (2016)	175
From *Please State the Nature of Your Emergency* (2017)	219
Index of Poems by Title	242

New Poems

Proposal

For this project I will hammer
a single finishing nail repeatedly
through individual pornographic paperbacks

then withdraw that nail and with what
words are pierced, verso, recto,
assemble an expletive- and typo-riddled

narrative, any missing letters indicated
with asterisks, the overarching and accidental
subject yet to be determined but likely extant

pleasures antique and contemporary religions forbid.
All grant monies will offset material costs
of nail, hammer, and books, estimated at $75,

plus millions for my ephemeral, irretrievable time.
For my next project I will slip and fall on several
personal injury law firms' stairs then sue for fortunes galore.

For my next project I will inhabit a bad mood
so many months and years it seems my proper dwelling.
Sufficient funding will permit me to explore

how best to monetize my gloomy emotional weather.
A content marketing campaign, maybe, with logo
and slogan on phone cases, T-shirts, water bottles, mugs.

For my next project I will enlist the assistance
of neighborhood birds, particularly
the persistent woodpecker, whose staccato

walloping of trees and houses resembles nothing
so much as a cop's knock, and reproduce
my first project but now with thin volumes of poems.

The beaks, odds run, will puncture empty space,
which poems on pages and all things mostly are.
Those burrowed blanks I'll document in photographs

and then enlarge to billboard dimensions for display
above our nation's population centers and roadways.
The working title for this project: *Messages from Beyond*.

What They Want the Poem to Do

Hector from lectern?
Offer nostrums from rostrum?
Spread like blood-borne pathogen?
Extrapolate from sorrow song?
Recollect and recast childhood trauma in prosaic phrases stacked in varying
    lengths?
As in tune on Spanish-language station float above comically bodily function tuba
    bass line falsetto pleading, "Mi corazon . . . mi corazon . . ."?
In our hearts replace for seconds at a time the rusty, crumbling structures—grain
    elevators, radio towers—with minuscule, gold-plated, cloud-shaped sculpture?
Create a playing card-size rainstorm constrained exactly to 52 drops?
Summon demon?
Portray Allah and invoke fatwah?
Project a hologram of Jesus weeping?
Squeal?
Squall?
None of the above. They don't want a poem at all.

How to Remove a Fishhook

Anchored in fat
pad of thumb or thin
skin of eyelid,
stranger's ear
or own lip, feed
the pronged barb
through, doubling
wound, followed
by lure and sinker,
line and pole, reel
and boat if boat
or dock or shore,
then body of water,
each dram and gallon
and plant and being
in pond or stream
or lake or sea
or ocean if need be.

Other Words

The administration regrets the error.
Events transpire hour by hour.

Data moves to the cloud in droves
from mobile devices and multiple drives.

Under the flooded island village spigot
pass mouths and bottles, jugs and buckets.

A change in the direction of curvature occurs
at the inflection point, which is not a cause.

At the inflection point, which is not a cause,
a change in the direction of curvature occurs.

Pass mouths and bottles, jugs and buckets
under the flooded island village spigot.

From mobile devices and multiple drives
data moves to the cloud in droves.

Events transpire hour by hour.
The administration regrets the error.

If/Then

If at dawn concentric
circles of sirens
ripple

between buildings,
over sidewalks,
litter, sleepers,

and the sun, new
old scold, makes no
reply,

the thinkable occurs.

If in my grandfather's Wisconsin
friend's garage hidden
skins, purloined pelts and hides
turned inside out, glistened,
how strange and sharp that night the stars.

For All the World

Sic transit gloria mundi
through Friday, Saturday, Sunday, so on.
Air gets wet and dirt roads muddy.
Worms eat birds and many hunger
Monday, Tuesday, Wednesday, then some.
You can never be too thin or rich,
never be too tall or handsome.
The banker's broke, the doctor's ill.
She felt fine at first and then unwell.
The body *is* a temple, damn it,
the mind a bright and vast cathedral.
If you don't like the weather, wait.
Windows warp and glaciers trickle.
If only we could fix a day in place.
If only we ran things, we think.
Sic transit gloria mundi
Friday, Saturday, Sunday, so on.

We All Have It Coming

Calculating the average age at which longevity experts expire
burns x-number calories an hour. How many oils and powders
to replenish the energy expended delaying the inevitable? Now
a freezing rain lacquers everything in the environs. Even leaves
and litter in gutters glisten. Say this for Anstett—saint and hero
of subjunctive, hypothetical suffering—were a hammer or base-
ball bat above his shiny, widening bald spot this instant, Anstett
would hire no one to suffer in his stead, whatever weather, not
just because he's broke and cheap. Good man. Brace yourself.

Bullseye

In the ammo factory, robots
sort and box the bullets
people drift to, bills of lading

slapped on every wrapped and ready pallet.
Even with abacus, calculator, computer,
I cannot total the world's abundant

antidotes to happiness nor in the form
of declarative sentences recreate the look,
sound, and smell of a Hong Kong alley

circa 1905, first midnight, then noon,
let alone conjure its spectral denizens.
Along the body's splashy corridors

lurk histories and afflictions, the opposite
of a dollop of suffering the standard condition.
But hummingbirds' little hearts beat

up to 1,260 times per minute, and a whale's tongue
can weigh as much as an elephant. Take that,
average bullet, traveling 2,500 feet per second.

Possible Report Made in Error

All of what happens goes on mostly not mattering.
From yonder I hear a holler and neither startle nor collapse.
The contraptions designed to stall if not stop time finally fail.
Given the many absences in our wake death makes plagiarists of us all.
Remember when we stood in swiftly rusting dusk before the bare fact of the
    famous empiricist's grave?
Where we wanted a certain glittering future instead there now lies along the
    horizon a thin and barely visible shim.
How weirdly eerie and suddenly other seem those things most familiar.
My name is Aaron Anstett and I fully understand the seriousness of the statements
    made in this declaration.

Plea

Alexa, help me
decrease my surface area
then go live in sepia-tone cabin
on the label of bottle of Bourbon
in imagined, idealized Kentucky,
never a slave state nor home
to continued mountaintop removal
but birthplace still of Abraham Lincoln,
Loretta Lynn, Harry Dean Stanton, Muhammed Ali.

Alexa, from the cross-hatched chimney
trickles a scribble of wood smoke,
and through a window you see a thin and tiny me
reading in rocking chair, bottle on table,
image on label infinitely repeating.

Alexa, how many days left, not mine alone but everyone's?

Alexa, what shall we do or say to lessen suffering?

Alexa, when will we at last infiltrate the kingdom of heaven?

Alexa, how do we gain immunity from prosecution for our many crimes and sins?

Alexa, how can I and the entire extended human family
enter witness protection but instead of southwest desert
or Midwest suburb, different, better planet and/or dimension?

Alexa, a hummingbird in the orchard swoops from apples to peaches.

Alexa, please.

Somewhere the Patch of Dirt Awaits

The objective correlative of when I cannot concentrate
remains a photograph of train tracks
seen from hotel window through snowstorm, spiderwebs
of parallel lines obscured by momentary flecks.
The backs of buildings—dumpsters and loading docks—
seen from trains remain a metaphor for what I cannot say.
I might calculate the total dollar value of everything
I ever shoplifted but who—*whom*, if picky—would I repay?
Until then, akin to the arcades Walter Benjamin described
before his suicide—younger than I am today—
I feel architected of iron and glass. Like his project,
I feel unfinished. I may have become a great text.

Mission

As in Zeno paradox we will never
cross a distance, stopping each
increasingly closer point halfway
between us and the final destination

to say "Thank you" to all the forces
delaying harm, drivers pausing
for lights and gargoyle cornices
firmly and sturdily affixed, grimaces

spitting rain when rain, wind when wind,
but not dropping on our blessed heads so far.
In the grand scale of the universe the hot
garbage and piss smell of a neighborhood

matters as much and little as vivid political
murals and soda logo and wax coating
on a sidewalk sleeper's wrinkled cup,
ransacked of money by unstoppable elements.

Immutable

1.
In accordance with the laws of physics, I blunder
toward the future the same rate as all things
living and dead. One grade school field trip
we visited the city jail. Inside a cell
door some hand had scratched, "Open."
I'd just turned ten and asked what happened
for birthdays and was laughed and laughed at.
"Not even a small cake?" I asked.

2.
Maybe one day we'll replace every Confederate general
statue with luminous ampersands, gold as uniform
buttons and epaulettes, wide as horse's ass and tall
as the gaunt and haunted figures for which they'll stand,
conjoining all in every direction, north to melting icecaps,
south to same, east to west and west to God knows where.

Some Clarifications

On many screens stock photographs
of the attractive collaborate around tables
with bespoke coffee and digital apparatus.

For X let's say "nearly infinity."
For pre-emptive obit errata forbid
"troubled," "loner," "caught
on camera," "scuffle."

Honestly, I've lied to you this entire time.

When dealing with difficult people, remember
it requires 62 muscles to frown
but only 26 muscles to smile,
32 psi to occlude the trachea
but just 4.9 for the jugular and carotid arteries.

"Because that's where the money is,"
Willie Sutton denied saying
in his autobiography when asked why
he robbed banks. "Why did I rob banks?
Because I enjoyed it. I loved it.
I was more alive when I was inside a bank,
robbing it, than at any other time in my life."

When we forget the words of hymns we hum.

Apparatus

Who will invent a bullet that mists
into pure, inert liquid on impact,

umbrella of minuscule flecks
clearer than distilled water, ricochets
and dead-on shots slapstick splashes

whatever surface, concrete and flesh?
Who, in the words of the prayer I recite

when speeding down runways, will feed
the hungry, house the homeless, heal
the sick, mend the broken? Who forgive

my many sins and perfect a procedure
to remove from memory everything awful,

earliest and most recent trauma, irresistible,
insistent refrains of terrible songs?
I fear I'd infect you if listing them.

You know the ones. They go *doo-da-doo-
da-doo* and *hey-hey-huh-huh* on and on and on.

Vast Gist

While so much burned we watched
pixels flicker on glossy surfaces.

I squandered hours I could have
spent otherwise (streaming wrestling

promos and spicy food challenges
instead of telling the people I love

I love them). With my eyes I followed
an ant to its nest then mapped with pencil

on paper its path. With my brain I supposed
one of every umpteenth wave fleetingly

mirrors the shape—ice sculpture's glassy
outline in air—of wave at its exact antipodes.

In my defense, the world looked like this
when I arrived. Mea culpa: I'm 2–4%

Neanderthal and no doubt some part
Genghis Khan in universe infinitely

unfolding origami. All appearances
we cannot fix much—even if we ceased

all fossil fuel use tomorrow, stopped
eating animals, cast every phone and gun

into long-dormant and smoldering volcanoes—
but let us name the fly that flew inside

an airplane from Orlando to Denver
last Sunday and occupied for many

of the 1,560 miles my attention, roosting
on headrest above seatback entertainment

screen, looking about and rubbing hands,
let us call that dignified stowaway something

noble as *Musca domestica: Maimonedes*
or *Pericles* or *Lofty, Setter of Records*.

Andre the Giant Has a Posse

André Roussimoff occasionally was driven
to school by Samuel Beckett, who lived
in the village. Grown, over seven feet tall,
he loved little more than being confined
in small spaces with friends and letting loose
extravagant, prolonged flatulence. Legendarily,
he often drank 100 beers in one go. All living
things suffer. What's animal in us scrabbles.
On any vicinity's periphery: junkyard, graveyard.
Maybe the vehicle rusts in a meadow.
Everything reminds me of something else.

Lorem Ipsum Flotsam Jetsam Harum Scarum Punctum Dictum Cockalorum

Wind troubles corrugated storage structures and makes
flagless chains clank against their poles all night and day.

Please be seated anywhere, grass or asphalt, and discern
the non-random pattern a single clanking chain creates.

A headline on my handheld says a program measures
art's entropy but cannot speed or slow decay.

Collage served as the 20th century's emblematic art form.
21st's? Security footage of museum selfie-takers destroying art.

While children froze and died in detention, we argued
whether a meditative, lyric poem implies a narrative.

For years I discovered new ways to be stupid
about basics of existence. Now I repeat them.

When I return as ghost, I'll be the sound
of dripping water traceable to no visible source.

Only an ordinary afterwards over which time and memory
apply lacquer as if thumbprint preserved on bannister.

One asleep in a gulley dreams the State gently
withers but first depicts genitalia on currency.

Follow the unbelievable true story of how we lived
millennia on a planet and left it uninhabitable.

Uninterrupted by objects, a projectile succumbs eventually to gravity.
Solution? Place between bullets and targets infinite distance.

Inside the cardboard box that holds a ceremonial plate,
suspended from fourteen threads three tiny spiders sway.

The river's first trickle's no wider than thimble under
gaunt wires cawing birds a brief season tenant.

Oceans encroach on shores; islands sink; a dormant disease
in reindeer carcass formerly veneered by tundra thaws.

Everything! Exists! At once! Nebulae! Roman statue granules! Waters!
Then! Yoink! One hand feeling another suddenly stops!

With seeming ease daylight begins as hint and scrim
and grows two-by-four emphatic, walloping here to yonder.

And the sunset looks resplendent—every orange and pink
and aquamarine—and belongs, vanishing, to us all.

The 99 Names of My Band

I'll name my band The Soylent Shakes.
I'll name my band The Cinnamon Clump.
I'll name my band Stale Yellow Light.
I'll name my band Sinister Chocolatiers.
I'll name my band Timely Hankering.
I'll name my band Screaming Extremists.
I'll name my band Formal Warning.
I'll name my band Shithouse Wedding.
I'll name my band Colossal Bonsai.
Adjective-Noun Construction.
Donkey Haughty.
Sancho Panzer.
Rosy Naughty.
Errors and Omissions.
Terminal Flibbertigibbet.
Vanishing Vanishing Point.
Where a Nickel Costs a Dime.
Cranky Baby.
I'll name my band The Uncle Whose Blood Type's Vodka.
Weary, Enabling Aunt.
Eight Ball, Coroner Pocket.
She Saw Stop Signs as Suggestions.
Exactly As Dumb As I Look.
Any Theories Why We're Here?
Rebutting All Evidence.
Cryogenic Suspenders.
Pasta Fiasco.
I'll name my band Big Honking Imbroglio.
Quote Unquote.
You May All Go to Hell and I Will Go to Texas.
On the Eighth Day God Regretted.
Imperative Form of the Verb "to Hear."
A Distant Whisper.
An Urgent Murmur.
The Wind Through Ash Heaps.
The Dress Hem's Swish.
I'll name my band Rattle of Cattails.
Pant Leg Thistle.
Rustle of Chain Link.
Eerie Warble.

Wheezing Then Weeping.
Fuzzy Thrum.
Incipient Tumult.
Bovine Ruckus.
Horse Hooves on Asphalt.
I'll name my band Intermittent Outcry.
Carnival Holler.
The New-Born Wails.
Meniscus Crackle.
Tendon Twang.
Oracular and The Ululations.
Staccato Hammer.
Detecting Patterns in Random Static.
Dry Beans in Pie Tin.
I'll name my band Tires on Gravel.
Rain Plops on Blue Tarp Someone's Roof.
Crack of Iceberg Calving.
Culminating Plunk.
Among the Trumpets, Ha, Ha.
You Call That Music?
Can I Get More Turmoil in My Monitor?
Setting the World's Record for Longest Band Name, Formerly Held by [Insert Name of Former World's Longest Band Name Record Holder Here].
Strategic Redaction.
I'll name my band ____ __ __ _____.
Labia Force Majeure.
Vas Deferens Librarian.
Scrotal Rodeo.
Anything with a Pulse.
Hickory Syrup.
Lucifer Hummingbird.
Slippery Slog.
Tra-La-Lump.
I'll name my band Sturm und Drab.
Hazardous Stupefactions.
Anti-Vaxxer Dope Slap.
Teetering Fringe.
Shudder to Imagine.
Darling, the Government and Corporations Don't Love Us.
If Only It Were Otherwise.
Subjunctivitis.
Gym Class Exercise: Play Dead.

I'll name my band Opposing Forces in Space-Time Proximity.
The Ouroboros Who Swallowed an Omphalos.
Forbidden Box of Human Misery.
Forever Reaching for Fruit and Water.
The Ninety-Nine Names of Allah.
That Which Has No Definition.
Me and Your Granny on Bongos.
Wee Hour Worries.
The Citizenry Stared at Screens.
I'll name my band Docile Constituents.
Extremest Weather on Record.
Send Notice to the Provinces: Waters Rise.
Extinction Event.
No Original Members.
Anaphora O.D.
All Words Ever Asymptotically Approach.
In Infinite Infinities Finite Finishes.
An End to All Endlessnesses.

Alas It Is So, But Thus It Must Be

Ira Louvin, drunk again,
smithereens his mandolin.

Bold to sin
if you believe it sin

and reckon heaven
real as Satan.

Years from then,
Charlie soloes, leans

from microphone
where Ira joined in.

The Sonnet Again Enjoys a Moment

The real and imagined seem opponents.
The world's first raspberry-picking robot
plucks the crop and gingerly deposits
it into punnets, plastic mesh baskets
for gathering vegetables and fruit.
The whole process takes about a minute
for a single berry. Modern sonnets,
on the ascendant, more and more wanted,
can be quickly transported to markets,
every apparatus running full tilt.
Of displaced labor the text keeps silent.
A poem tries to make things equivalent:
harvests and fixed forms, couplets and hilltops.
Miniature suns glimmer in dew drops.

Can't Get There from Here

The best of wrestling's when the wrestlers yell
into microphones just how and how much
they'll hurt their enemies. Now paradise might be
an empty threat or leisurely breathing
anywhere, hospital or jail cell, hours
on end, luxuriating in the air.
Even this late I believe I'd still feel
at home riding town to town on Greyhound,
for seatmate newly sprung convict who talks
at length about his fears his wife's a cheat.
As we neared our destination, northern
California, he grew increasingly
anxious. I overheard him on a phone
saying how he loved her, how he'd hurt her.

He Do the Polysemy in Different Voices

Scarcely had the evening settled when a ravaged man
in doorway nearer than you'd imagine yelled,
"I'm comfortable as bell or clapper, cause of some alarm."

In a bag he's stockpiled buttons and slot machine handles
in service of what purpose he'll only darkly mumble,
maybe satiric political art or apocalyptic machine.

In the vicinity of rivers he grows drowsy inexplicably.

He's come to believe a sacredness adheres
to pursuing the absurd, to wit his "Canticle for Cuticles"
recited on public transport and in government offices.

Find the sacred texts on library shelves
in which painstakingly he's swapped each scriptural "and"
for handwritten curlicues of ampersands.

"I will live inside this body even if and/or until it kills me,"
I suspect a not-too-distant me demands.

As a people we enthuse about the metaphoric and actual
transformation of caterpillar to chrysalis then butterfly,
but few exclaim it equally meteoric if grubbier and grimmer
when maggots transpire to houseflies, rise from purely crawling
things to zig-zag and harry the rented air.

I will live inside this dunderheaded body even if and/or until it kills me.

If only to have been an artificer of antiquity's automatons,
devices so uncanny the father and son inventors
landed in prison as suspected magicians.

Costly Repairs

How splendid not to be nor to have been
Edgar Allan Poe, drunk and hungry,
self-defeating, or cadaverous drifter
hitching quickly as possible to the next town.

Moot wilderness survival advice: Attacked
by dinosaur, act like asteroid. Anomalous
oceanic conditions shift food sources,
resulting in more and more gray whales

washing ashore. I woke nostalgic
for my childhood rust-belt river town's
smell of creosote and fish. Overheard
while waiting for library to open, "I want

a burger with double cheese" then, "Girl,
no money means no food!" What to whisper
in the dying's ears and evoke soothing eucalyptus?
In the novel's tavern a drunkard with tankard

talks awkwardly. Backwards fly the seconds.
Little, I believed I'd split atoms tearing paper fast.
The order of the Roman alphabet's a mnemomic
for spelling *Mnemonsys*, goddess of sacred memory.

Other than living tree or stump the earth
possesses few good places to find an ax embedded but plenty
to see the vague impression of a human face:
tree bark, oil stain, grasses on which frost creates a lace.

Some Final Statements

In conclusion, the onset of sunset tinted
windows and faces, the to and fro of everything,
waters in their beds and cradles, the various vessels we toss and rest in.

In conclusion, I read that our generally dumbass representative
voted to defend public broadcasting and felt briefly hopeful,
but he voted to "defund."

In conclusion, an invisible and immaterial lace
seemed to settle across the breadth and width of landscapes,
the warp and woof of surfaces.

In conclusion, animals left or returned to their burrows,
nests, hives, and dens, not one worried
about the afterlife or money.

In conclusion, a headline made me happy, *The Brains
of Birds Synchronize When They Sing
Duets*. It did not last.

93% of Statistics Wither Under Scrutiny

Take all the world's scuffed and threadbare surfaces,
cardboard houses in Toy District of Los Angeles,
one example. Take all the world's glittery instances,

single pixel of Shibuya billboard currently
lush speck of actor's eyelash. Take the world turning
into somewhere else. All the room in the universe,

n-dimensional, mostly the upshot's oops.
The plow that carves the earth and turns,
reverses course, obverse, inverse, continues

to exist abandoned in meadow, hammered to atoms,
transformed to swords. The definition of "nebulous"
remains difficult to define. A winter coat cannot be lost

and retrieved from dream nor can dollars or song.
Were God holding forth in tavern, who'd hear?
In winter an exhale and whistle silver the air.

Just to Change the Subject for a Second

Can I ask you a question beyond this question?
Is existence a flicker between two mysteries, as in parable of sparrow in mead hall?
Show of hands, who hears the future, rumbling like engines?
Who hears the past, that vast silence?
Imagine skeletons in Victorian finery, shushing boisterous child skeletons in same.
Imagine skeletons in togas debating the weight of the soul.
Imagine skeletons in battle gear resting between attacks.
Imagine skeletons in no clothes at all.
Doing so, let us set the world's record for sloth and fecklessness.
Let us posit a supreme being commensurate with the run-on sentence of
    persistence, energies swapping around.
The tempus sure as heck fugits, bless it.
Sooner fire bullets at clouds or rockets at the sun as petition The Ineffable for
    recompense to replace all lost things and make us whole.
Sooner sass the air or interrogate an empty chair. Sooner fistfight ghosts.
Sooner demand quiet in a catastrophe of choiring sirens.

From *Sustenance* (1997)

Pharmacy

If, at the pharmacy, I say to the woman
frowning behind the counter, "My heart's
a bad check, make good on it," will that mean
a kind of November has settled in my blood

and I'll be ready then to never lie again?
If, with my change, she offers me matches,
will she want to live with me forever
and together we'd love everything we touched?

"I'm no good for you," I'd say, holding the flame
just under my cigarette. Then, like some tough guy,
I'd breathe in hard, pulling the fire up.
If I lit it first try, would things work out between us?

Would she give me a pill that could keep me from yelling,
"We're all dying! Help!" in emergency rooms for fun?
Would she have another we could split?
Would we find our way back to the world

inside this one, and our pure happiness catch on
with the druggist, who'd start crazily ringing
his mortar and pestle? As we linked arms at the exit,
wouldn't he give us that music for our wedding?

Man Saves Own Life

In the morning, before breakfast, I save my own life,
then walk around the house all day a hero.
Friends come by and ask how it feels.
I say it just happened. I couldn't help it.
They'd do the same in my shoes. I don't tell them how,
before I knew it, something raced down my fingers
and my feet. Something made me strong.
It crowded itself in my arms and my heart
and filled me up with as strange and kind a feeling
as I could remember, and suddenly I knew nothing
but I had to help that guy. It wasn't words. No voice
told me. It was more like light behind my eyes, weight
pressing in from every direction. High notes pierced me,
and it was clear what I had to do:

Claw

The big-time wrestler Baron von Claw
fought normal the first couple rounds
and should have lost. He was older, and his belly showed
under his tights. He had to be fifty, a little, fat guy
who got thrown around. But something always happened

across his face. Done for, his eyes changed,
pushed out of their sockets a bit and widened
like stains. About to be pinned, he'd be let up. Ali Baba,
Texas Jack, these powerful men would just unhand him,
simply stop fighting as the Baron stood upright,

and look around, nervous, and inch away backwards.
It was then, always, that the camera zoomed in
on the Baron's lips, which trembled a long time
before he said the word *Claw*. "Claw," he'd say,
"Claw," and next to his grin the Baron's right hand

would flash up, menacing, all five fingers cramped
and hideous, tips pointed straight at the camera
and the whole screen full of those tips.
When the camera pulled back, the Baron would start staggering
behind his claw, as if it led him. He took his time

pacing the ring. Even the announcers never blamed
King Henry, Mr. Insane, for giving in, for begging and cowering,
blubbering "No, No," as the claw descended. It did bad things.
It made a man nothing. The Baron himself would black out in spasms
if, before it went, he clasped his hands together, champion.

A Possible Reprieve

How much weeping right now into telephones,
or fistfights in lit rooms, both faces
panicky, how many people holding
their heads in their hands, afraid of going

a little crazy, and then a lot?
Who's picking a gun up again
and again, not sure, or staring hard
out the window, as if words

were appearing there,
and they are, in no order,
over the roofs and the cars,
in the middle of the air?

Wet Floor

> *We are currently investigating your employment history and assets for possible legal action.*
> —Collection agency letter

What can an honest man like Anstett tell his creditors
but, "Get in line. I've been in trouble with my woman
and the police. My brilliant stint as dustmop jockey
began with *garbage*, my first word, and, ambulatory as anything,
I strode the few rooms of my parents' first apartment, crowing
'Garbage, garbage,' a diapered little ragman, clearing
all clutter in my grasp: house keys, loose cash,
and emptied my hands above the kitchen trash can.
Bigger, I rolled a cradle in which my newborn
brother slept, blanket drawn across his head,
to where the back-porch steps began, three floors
up in the wind, or so my mother says. The cobbler's children
go unshod. Where I live now I leave a mess: beer cans,
and ashtrays, and open windows scattering drafts like this,
but you should see me following brooms through warehouses
from Oakland to Houston or sorting oily rags
for an industrial laundry in Kalamazoo. I dazzle my bosses.
'Never so orderly,' or some such, they chortle, from quit job
to new one. I've pressed my whole weight
on a buffer to slide right, lifted to scrub left, mixed the secret
cleaning agents in a yellow bucket marked *WET FLOOR*
and wheeled it down a corridor, work clothes filthier
by the minute, swept a just-swept stockroom, shaving seconds
off the time clock, cashed my paycheck and gone back for more.
Sirs: my employment history's a string of ill-fitting uniforms,
dirty jokes over smoke breaks, and W-2 forms, bleached feet
and mop-handle calluses. I own little no one's owned before:
that chronology of scratchy, rented, too-large pants, or the name,
sometimes ironed, sometimes stitched, on the always loose,
blue shirts, a few of which I stole as remembrances
and to augment the sociopathically clear eyes my driver's
license wills to anyone. Their color, too, is handed down
from who knows who, like my furniture and books
and every atom in my person, or the wallet all the money's
slipped in and out of, my grandfather's once, sure,
but a walking cow's one skin before. I remain sincerely yours."

Heaven

> *I will clamber through the Clouds and exist.*
> —Keats, *Letters*

Stepladders at fireworks, he explains, help eliminate
the middleman, the sky between the lights' flare
and his eyeballs. He's that much closer,

perched, to the sulfur, corneas nearer
the sizzle and spill. "On a dance floor,
I don't want to move my body, that vehicular

spectacle, just proclaim my thanks and glee,
afterwards, in bed. Any restaurant, I want already
to be full. Here, I'd forfeit the ghastly for the ghost,

the shadow for its source, and climb
the standby hook and ladder
past the cyclone-fenced restricted zone.

I will clamber through the clouds and exist,
the flashing din and nimbus a neighbor.
I could stand and face it, but, astride a high rung,

I turn to make out the faces, some giddy
and soft as a family's, grinning around the cake,
or wearing the bleary, livid shock of last call.

One of those expressions might be yours.
A look spreads across your face of concern
as you see me backlit and distant.

Imagine me then as looking into the open face of heaven.
Pretend it's weeks ago, before you've met me.
No one's yet prepared the fairgrounds.

I'm practicing balance in the backyard,
my own height off the earth.
Between bursts, think of the quiet, the lyrical, wind."

Slow Learners

We imagine the octopus knows
nothing of his three hearts or how
some day they'll give out, one by one.
When the eyes are closed, the eight legs done
curling up like pilots who pass out
at those high altitudes, the hearts take turns
getting cold. What a horrible thing to think
all day and night of the octopus
and his three hearts in his fat head.
They keep to themselves mostly,
but sometimes whisper answers
to each other like children
in a school for slow learners.

The Barber

> *Of death*
> *the barber*
> *the barber*
> *talked to me*
> —William Carlos Williams

The barber and I become so intimate
behind plate glass, through which turned faces
and slow, glittering cars pass, he's recommending ointments
and listing the things there ought to be laws for.

He trims around my ears, careful not to nick them.
He lays the skin of my neck bare with clippers.
I'm made nervous by the cuts on his knuckles.
Combs stand upright in jars of blue liquid.

Across the way, display-window mannequins
hold themselves firmly at the elbow and chin.
Except that I pay him, we're two men talking
with ease and assurance, as if neither of us ever

sat struck stupid with terror and grief.
Outside, a car honks. The barber, my new friend,
spins me in the chair. He brings his shaved cheek close.
Both of us beam at my handsome, handsome face.

This Street, Any Street

I could live here forever
but I'm not living forever.
Ask my kidneys. Ask the stitch

worrying my ribs, and my laboring lungs,
and my blood that runs. I say a needle's stuck
in my dead arm some day, blood let from me.

Or else I'm ashes, mixed in with other ashes,
a bit of bone, an uncrushed tooth.
Or never found, and disappearing

in a ditch. The surprise of my hands
alive in the morning, that's what I love,
working a cigarette from its pack

to show my body who's boss.
Nobody's heartache yet, I wring
a little wiggling from my fingers. I roll

my head around on my neck, its stem.
I walk to the kitchen window
and stare out at the sun.

Lessons

Cigarette plastered to my stupid expression,
I announce, "I'm taking cello lessons,
the most sorrowful of instruments.

I'll be the most diligent of students.
Believe me, when I say sorrow
dwells in the rooming house of my heart,

I don't mean part-time. It rants and snorts.
Day in and out, it paces the floorboards."
She pries into my musical background,

so I fieldstrip the burnt-out end,
scrap and ashes lilting in a slight wind
that spreads and settles them across the grass.

When all have fallen, I exclaim,
"You've heard, perhaps, that barechested,
tattooed Anstett's a crackerjack

accordionist, a prancing squeezebox man,
who capers in his kitchen, feigning
real playing by whistling 'Lady of Spain.'

Mornings, he works his makeshift concertina,
a fanned and folded front page
cut into silhouettes of children

holding hands. Between his hands,
this paper doll contrivance
contracts and expands. Song," I add, "is the universal. . ."

when she interrupts, "That's a far cry. . ."
"One of these days," I cry,
"I'm sawing on a violin for real,

blade slicing through the fine
handcrafting, deepest string twanging
for the last time first." I tuck

my chin to my chest to demonstrate. "This severing,"
I say, "rises in pitch," then run west
from her porch, the direction my imaginary handle points.

The Ticket Taker Speaks

The Boy With Big Hands, Lop-Sided Man,
who are these freaks? *The Flying If-Only's,
Mr. I Don't Know Who I Am?* Where's a singing
horse at least, a clever-with-numbers dog?
Woman Who Can't Love, Wrong In The Head?
And no snake tamer, no hypnotist around?
One platform diver, falling storeys
into a barrel, climbing out whole,
calm as he towels off, that's a show,
but here it's *Every Day's A Struggle*.
Look at him go. Here's his painstaking
wait in line, his startling dry eyes.
*Madame Sarah, Teller Of Half Truths, Worried
Bob?* And me, me, angry in the yellow light
of the ticket booth, with a slot I talk through
and another I use to slide back stubs. I tear
your ticket in half. I see my face cast in the glass.

Cusp

Red wine early leaves our mouths
wanting more, pink roofs tensing
for extra, hungering toward some bonus

wash and singe along our tongues.
Here in the world little
isn't labor: lifting one last glassful

afterwards, or before, bottle half full,
drawing the blinds, and in that forgery
of evening, that crepuscular sham,

deviling our nerve ends
all afternoon, axons jittery and lit.
You be the monster, I'll be scared,

then we'll switch back, as watch hands reel
above their gears across the planet
and waves pratfall on pestered shores.

Elsewhere, oleanders, venomous and lush,
stiffen in wind, where jackrabbits vanish
into the cactus, under a blue

and urgent atmosphere, in which stars,
dating back before records,
verify light's stubborn streak.

We're lodged inside this life
and could blunder into tomorrow dead,
easily as cattle lying down on their sides.

We're inexorably descending
in our skins. Generations of skeletons
sped here, where we localize leagues

of jerkwater kin. Our work for today
is finishing wine enough to run
yelling out to the yard, and the tree, where birds

will break and break from its limbs.
You know like them panicked best, unpeopling
branches, proving gravity wrong in droves.

Menace

> *It is the devil's ABCs.*
> —X, "True Love"

Menace starts small: a rubber hand
in the teacher's drawer, palm up, as if begging money
to be sewn back on, Washington's eyes

x'd over on the portrait near the chalkboard.
Voice deepening, you make emergency calls
to doctors' houses, claiming shooting

pains, your heart in something's grip.
Your father's office is called every payday
or so, some kid screaming, "I quit." No one's the wiser

the gasoline funneled from your sister's car
goes to fill neighbors' mailboxes, that it's you
who tapes twenty matchsticks to their lids.

Periscope rigged to the dash, you drive slouched
through nearby towns, as though the car propelled itself,
made corners, then parked in front of motels

where you register the names of wanted felons.
Then, your job at the novelty
factory folds. You've terrified your co-workers

into moving states away. Ticking lunch boxes.
Black water in the cooler. Off the record,
your foreman whispers, "The whole works is haunted."

A St. Paul bus station's where you're arrested,
wiring death threats to yourself. "I didn't mean it,"
you insist, "I wasn't about to carry through."

Measure of Revenge

It seems I long to stand
on the circle of floor sawn out
by crafty cartoon characters,
hand tools in their paws,
and descend, dumbfounded, sputtering
mumbo jumbo, intact but flabbergasted,
inch by inch unfinished basementward,
necktie fluttery in front of my nose.

My friends the animals gape and pop-jaw
as I bounce back in new, pressed suit,
dirty face and hands firm proof of where I've been,
ready to regale and reassure with stories
of victory over ancient and bitter quarrels,
like my dispute with such elemental lacks
as absence of trapdoors and the failure of magic
or science to explain all natural phenomena

as hypnotism: tsunamis and sunsets,
gene replication and smoke's hen scratching
explicable by the sway of suggestion
and spells objects seem heir to.
With *trompe l'oeil* tattoos and topiary hairdo,
I lug my environs elsewhere, through continuous frames
and constant comeuppances. These pet-store omnivores
commit jackassery unpunishable by law.

Physics

Collision: two objects attempting to exist simultaneously in space and time.

Every book a copy, this blue sky's a constant
fabrication, and the sheet of glass I watch
for slip-ups through, for holes in the story
to emerge, jittery as television static,
with excited ions engaged in connivance,
lets in the persistent, glittering world,
sun sparing little on faces that glide
above the sidewalks on stealthy necks or plot
through windshields the least dangerous route.
O citizens of my surveillance, last night you slept
and dreamed strange, walking alphabets of satiety
and loss, eyes jerky beneath their lids. I guess you did,
who didn't get a wink in and would like right now
some knockout pills and beer. We're uttered
into flesh, and then reiterated, senselessly miraculous,
like the pulse I could find in my arm this instant,
or the housefly exploiting my tolerance, who uncoils
in the kitchen, lending this a whit of credibility.
Film of me looking stupid in line with my purchases
erases in a liquor store's back room, or video,
in which I'm a series of digital emissions, buying
Bloody Mary mix and Slim Jims. I'm a respite
in a run of no customers, an enhancing of the action.
I'm replaced in every bus seat I vacate. Exposure
slow enough, any photograph's a palimpsest. That's how
we're made: scintilla spin. Routes overlap.

Small Favors

The detective opens his eyes first thing,
ambulanced by sun, thanks God the rent's paid
and his window's not a ganglia of cracks
like the windshield of the Pontiac he'll stare through
all day to afford to fix. He's tired of the pieced-out

picture, of putting bits together, and who would blame him
to his face? *Nothing*, he says, *adds up for long,
and if a client gets the answer they want, it's just
more proof of something wrong. Why go looking
or pay someone to look?* He's tired of stakeouts,

so many motel parking lots, afternoons
waiting for the spouse to leave with no luggage
and no idea they're being watched. The detective dragasses
out of bed, lighting cigarettes end to end, fuses
the spent and full. *There's a life*, he says, *one comes to

have no cure for.* Small favors, but he's glad his place
is close enough to hear the tollway, that rush he thinks
means *out*. He stretches a little, then rises up to look
across 14th, to his office above the currency exchange
and liquor store, the one whose sign says *All types

of government checks cashed here*. He's tired
of tracking stubs. Like keys for gas-station bathrooms, chained
to plastic coffee mugs, something obvious and less loseable,
the detective thinks we're evidence of angels, them of us.
He thinks a body's chalk outline's the imprint of a nimbus.

Hoopskirt Parish

I blame the narcoleptic aerialist,
who walks the wire in fits and starts,

traipsing along and suddenly stalled,
swaying in the big top's attic,

threatening any moment he'll interrupt the air.
I blame him for interrupting himself, blame him

for losing track, as if the air's God's
wandering church, as if he's skipping services.

It might be his inching's a fast and a harvest.
When he comes to his senses, all at once

awake and gasping, scared as the almost drowned,
he might be ready to quit fooling around.

Lackadaisical at great heights,
he doesn't halve and halve the remaining stretch

to make it take forever, doesn't speed things up
between the platforms. He keeps sleeping on his feet,

balanced on that span, keeps nodding off
above no net. His act's an employment

record, full of gaps. And he's his own boss.
And he keeps getting his old job back.

Evenings Full of Forfeiture

Take me. My yes to a whiskey, no
to a ride home, belief the wind thickens
across slight birds and the thinly clothed,
my sudden desire to roll on the ground,
cut across the face by stones,
to turn my pockets out and walk
through a field at dusk,
singing hymns and hillbilly songs,
to be held for questioning, then beaten
to paste and that paste to dust
that rises without memory and makes bail,
to drive from dark to dark,
fingers seizing in work gloves.
Take me, breaking dollars into parts,
coins to last, quick drinks.
Take the evenings, bluing to black
unstoppably past gas pumps
and beyond my seeing to heating grates
and houses. Take it on faith
whether you wake or not, dawn
italicizing the obvious:
world still here, easy target
for our bodies and rain
falling miles. Say amen, someone.

Sustenance

I want to be pulled down the street
by thousands of finches, each
with a twine leash, nothing fancy,
one block only, through the brazen afternoon.
Hopping and walking, they'll haul me
easily. I'm a thin man, who'll whoop

on his toy sled, pitching bread scraps
ahead of them, their skinny legs a blur.
True to my word, I'll halt at the corner,
unbridle each bird, and each will fly off
with its own string, my blessings on their nests.
I've half a mind to weigh so little

I balance in one hand, my grandfather's, say,
suddenly alive again. I want to feel so good
it's a faith I take with me, like food
or money. A sound I can count on, keen
as metal runners rasping asphalt.
A prayer I say and the birds return.

Five Definitions

These days, when it seems I can no longer live
in just one body, it's hard to remember
being so crowded in I might have been
the three rooms a widow stays in all winter
to save on heat, farmhouse tougher and tougher
to keep with taxes. *Magnanimous* does not mean
the soul enlarging literally, swerving out
and headed directions. I thought it did. I run circles
around myself and call that space the generous yard
I might have grown up in. Someone, please, short hairs
from around my temples have come undone and landed
on this page you'll read some further version of.
By then, who knows, my wiry, alcoholic arms might lift
a skinny window in my New Brunswick kitchen, sill
a chopping block in the works, but no, nothing much
bad will happen as I stick out my more-bald head to check
what day it's turning into: Thursday and hurricane weather
or Monday stopped still in a warm spell. Climates shuffle
around like that, fast, when one body's not enough.

Blur

You're grieving a blue streak
over the disappearing present,
and there it goes, another yawn
floating up in you like heat, the way you swear
prayers rise. Down there, a city worker spills
shovel after shovel of tar onto the street
and tamps it, a stopgap until the street again
unfreezes. It's freezing by your window,
where you shake to tatters, watching his breath
smear the air, a blur of atoms, and you're sick
of the unseen, of the casual air
the city worker has, him with his blueprints
exacting every rod in the curbing, though you
could be so much in love with him your fears
would put themselves in order, a catalog
of birds. You almost want him to catch you
looking down, the way you dunced around
a Goodwill once, stealing a used
anatomy book. You wanted to know how
we look inside, systems overlapping
on the see-through pages, a peel-away
atlas. You hoped the clerk knew the book
was under your coat and were ready to explain
it all to him: how tired you were of no proof,
of every second exiting like music, which goes
with hardly any evidence. Even at closing
he said nothing, and you almost confessed,
then stood past dark in your building's lobby,
facing the stairs. Glass door behind you,
you trusted anyone looking in would see
how the streetlights sketched a shadow
of the *ENTRANCE* sign across your back.

Open Beer Stores, Running Buses, Marigolds Small Miracles on Police Station Lawns

Who thought the day went on, sewn of whole cloth,
over working hours, beyond the factory floor,
past hints the break-room windows and glimpses
the twin bay doors allowed, when you were suffered
a cigarette, or the conveyor belt emptied, briefly moving
nothing but itself, or machinery broke, and looking up
you saw out: sunlight, beguiling, and the jerky color film
called *Leaves* the trees broadcast, and a frame of sky
with birds enough its entirety went assumed?

Who'd guess it so extensive, so uncannily blue,
and the world full of such expensive views,
when you've up and walked off, still on the clock,
right under the noses of your new former bosses,
not even trotting the old saw "I quit" out,
or invoking some commotion of screaming and thrown parts,
but turned and took a certain number of steps
across the concrete, on through the gravel lot,
almost disappointed no one cried, "Come back"?

Absentee, no one's employee, fodder for gossip,
last check owed you, cause of production lull
as someone's made to man your position, who knew
it got this good, before acquiescing to want ads
and dialing phone numbers for addresses
you'll drag your whole and only body to, your hands,
minutes ago lifting 7,200 parts per hour, hieing you home,
steering like victory, and later, drinking liquor on principle,
being able to lie down and rest at will, whether you do or no?

Labor

To wake each smudged morning, ready or not,
and set both feet down, to stand
in the one body allowed you, the life
whose days run to equal shares light and dark,
to wash your face and walk to the table
where you eat breakfast because you must,
to clean your plate and point your fork,
"This is the ceiling, this the floor,"
to rinse the same shirt nightly in the kitchen sink,
name you're known by stenciled above its pocket
as you run past houses, dogs loud in the yards,
to punch in before the line starts and go smoke
in the break room, listening to troubles
and extravagant swear words
repeated so often they begin to sound dull,
to work six shifts until Sunday, and, afraid
of falling asleep in church, stay home
that day and rub your arms, to have a drink
in the early afternoon, just a touch
of something see-through in your glass, some vivid
strong liquor you drink slow to make it last.

Shift

A little snow blew in where we stood.
Our boots squared off at the toe.
The doctors, said John Flowers,
didn't know fuck-all. Surgery
worsened something in his daughter.

John Flowers spat his cigarette
between the trailer and the bay door,
squinted his eyes and lit another.
He asked me if I'd ever killed a man.
All I wanted was a pallet

of certain-size parts unloaded
so I could run them to the floor.
He scratched his stomach, said he had,
one punch to that man's solar plexus,
back in Missouri, an accident. *I boxed*,

he said, and made me feel the arm.
He made me say I believed him.
Management could kiss his ass.
They weren't paying towards her bills.
He'd drive his forklift drunk or sober.

Hell if I wouldn't, he whispered,
holding me in a bear hug. *Some days,
son of a bitch*, he said, *it's like losing your wallet
and there's no proving who you are anymore.*
Close to my ear he called me *Kid*.

Bare Lot

The rubble buildings make of any sky's
an interruption, fixed and jagged stance
asserting permanence as daylight dies
along it, or the present weather hints,
in flecks and streaky rills, at shifty threats.
I like a bare lot sometimes, city blocks
of them, blank spaces left like unpaid debts
where wrecking balls or fire leveled stacks
and stacks of offices. You see the air
up in the air, newspaper blowing through,
unpinned from fences, sunshine, here, and there,
in patches, unobstructed, looking new.
I like the stripped-down feel of a place
made flat. You see day fill what night's erased.

Mississippi Delta Blues Musician's Picture Altered on Commemorative Stamp Presents More Positive Image

> *Me and the devil was walking side by side.*
> *I'm going to beat my woman until I get satisfied.*
> —Robert Johnson, "Me and the Devil Blues"

Robert Johnson died young, strychnined whiskey
someone's jealous husband slipped him down south,
sang he'd use a pistol, "cut her half in

two." His Postal Service stamp, the pesky,
famous cigarette's erased. His fix-mouthed,
grave face travels, stripped, through towns where he'd been

known for fleeing hellhounds, drink, and playing
blues so charged and stark some devil must have
got his signature in blood. The fraying
document holds up because I just have

forty and one hundred syllables, near
flawless trochees. Bones in time get picked dull.
Johnson phoning agent: "This woman here
said she'd pleasure me. I lacks a nickel."

Worry

Say you want to sing right now,
over and over, the name of an old lover.
Aren't you afraid the neighbors will hear
your voice shaking a little, the way you shook
in that lover's arms, the night you started
losing one another? If you were me, you felt
a lessening no talking could lessen, a sense
the motel television made sense just then,
with its wash of poorly adjusted color
lighting the room. Between leaving
for more ice and forcing a toast
to the future, plastic glasses patting
and sloshing, you thought, "This
is what we're entitled to."

If, unlike me, you had pulled the curtains open,
overhead lights might have glinted
off the balcony railing for you
and exposed the courtyard, the shutdown
fountain. The two of you might have danced
down there, slowly and close. The two of you
might have rescued something beautiful.
If you were me, you wouldn't sing
that name either. You'd worry
about the neighbors. You'd worry like I do.

Why Skylines

Because the sky is a dumb show without them.

Because the plains terrify, end to end,
with what could cross them toward us,
huge against no background.

Because we'd stand guard,
work in shifts to dot the landscape,
and never lie down together.

Because we lie down on your bedroom floor
and let the sun spend hours dying
across our faces and the hills and buildings.

Because we don't rise
to turn a light on, we're that calm,
we trust a skyline not to vanish if we stop believing.

Tell Me

Do I tell my daughter it's a goodly huge world,
a hard place, but the only one
with Chinese carry-out, or that, waiting in line,
her father's convinced the latest gunman,
some exhausted loner, will send us to heaven?
Do I say this life is beautiful and dangerous,
a red dress soaked in gasoline?
That some moments in it hold, or build
with majesty like music, erasing all anguish,
while others, without meaning,
foist themselves on us like a fraud?
That our bodies are real, and hurt,
and our minds go irreparably wrong,
as if we willed into being what we most fear?
O Lambs-eat-ivy, it's magic and catastrophic here.
Light enters the eyes
and bounces like bullets in a concrete room.

Mercy

God, in whom I do not wholly trust,
whose evidence glares over the terrible earth,
may the deaths of everyone I love

stay for them abstract, like ground must seem
for some time to the parachutist:
general and pale, not actual, but map,

whose scale increasingly closes in on 1:1,
each grass blade, dirt clod, small stone
looming life-size and clarified at last.

From *No Accident* (2005)

Afterlife

Perhaps the four-color photograph of a lube stop and car wash,
like a heaven above the numbered days and months of a giveaway calendar,

is heaven and shall be our dominion forever, with glare on the glass doors
and lettering spelling something. Maybe the man with indistinguishable features

standing on a sidewalk runs things, and those driving vehicles somewhere
for eternity: heaven's emissaries, the interrupting angels, who veer

from this to that world. In the few scraps blown in after the asphalt was swept
and the pyramid of mortared cannonballs in the park off the highway,

where the swings hang absolutely still, as if painted there, we find our joy always.
And there, on the photograph's left edge, the birds eternally arriving.

History

No one in this world remembers making love in 1648,
though somebody must have, maybe everyone did,

or recalls the exact angle to which a sparrow bent a pine branch afterwards,
shaking loose a little rain nestled in the needles there,

or can say with any certainty what that sounded like,
whether breath, or skin against skin, or nothing.

Drinks

In taverns named for dire conditions,
On a Bender, Eighty-Sixed, Thirsty Sharks,

Jackson sat long and drank from dawn to dark.
Night monotoned the standard rendition:

slow to quick drinks, brief grace to perdition.
Day starts with bird song, ends in dog barks.

Who sleeps well tonight in public parks?
Jackson awoke in awkward positions:

doorways, cocaine traced across cracked, glass plates,
week's pay, rain-wet; someone's shower stall;

who's-its porch swing; what criminal's couch?
Names on newsprint caught in sewer grates

stay names. The orbits survive us all,
and that bad tosspot Jackson's head hurts. Ouch.

❊

That bad tosspot Jackson's head hurts. Ouch.
Light pours all over him. He cannot last.

His face his father's, the sun a real bastard,
Jackson believes he's what rough beast slouches

toward Bethlehem. Watch, watch, watch, watch, watch:
he walks by the mirroring storefronts fast,

avoids his own eyes, little fright mask
stuck on the skull in which his wet brain's sloshed.

Get this man some vivid, strong liquor quick.
Too bad he's spent his literal last cent

this morning on a pack of cigarettes.
He lights one with a tavern match and flicks

it out. Go find it on that sidewalk, bent
by Jackson's fingers, alive, though he forgets.

※

Jackson's fingers (alive, though he forgets)
touched everything he touched: dying hands,

newborns, miles of skin, tossed contraband,
acres of pages, dirt, milk-swollen breasts,

but these they cradle and remember best:
beer cans, bottles, their lids and glass, the strand

of printed paper on the whisky's cap and
maker's labeled promise and forced health threats.

Jackson's poured vodka into paper cups
with a little vermouth and served himself.

He's used his own fingers to mix a drink.
They don't shake. Sobriety interrupts

him often. He's still as a coastal shelf.
Jackson's OK. He's functioning. He thinks.

※

Jackson's OK. He's functioning. He thinks,
"Sunrise over China. Great God above.

The grand plant life alcohol is made of
circumscribes the world, its blossom and stink

rich in the villages where small birds blink,
and large birds, and none. Those flowers and fluff:

ancestors set some out to rot and loved
what happened: dizzying liquid that links,

it seems, man to God, Jackson to bigger
being. This wash washes all, erases

last night's mistakes, bathes tomorrow's sorrows.
Pain in the world is too much to figure.

Who first? Which town? What evidence, traces
of crushing ancestry, grief Jackson knows?"

NO ACCIDENT

❈

Of crushing, ancestral grief, Jackson knows
this much: too much. He'd rather tie one on.

That's why bars open early, the reason
neon's lit in daylight, how money goes

so swiftly, and why the many zeroes
of bottles' mouths yawn on until stark dawn.

Jackson drinks at each drink until it's gone,
orders more, drinks until the swollen scene shows

through his magnifying glass: fast bar clock,
dimmed and brightened faces, shelved bottles lined

in drunken alphabetical order.
Patsy Cline plays on every jukebox

he can think of. Jackson asks the closed blinds,
"Ever have a morning eye-opener?"

❈

"Ever have a morning eye-opener,"
asks Jackson, "lose a day, suffer blackouts?"

Ever cower while a woman shouts
at another through the locked apartment door

and calls your name and calls you a liar
or walk heel-toe as a policeman doubts

you're sober? Ever rummage for and count
each coin in the house then go buy liquor?

Hard to stack them drunk. Hard to come up short
at a counter and argue with the clerk

you'll bring the rest by soon. Ever see men
ask for one free one from the gleaming quart

they state at instead of the man at work
behind the bar? They know it won't happen.

※

Behind the bar, they know it won't happen:
drinks pouring themselves, humorous phrases

carved in wood pointing a way, their faces
suddenly those on currency or thin

and young in the mirror. Light won't begin
shining from their eyes, lighting the places

they look and illuminating graces
each thought the others lost. Still, they drink in

drink on drink as if something were revealed.
It seems what is seen there cannot be told

until one begs one more drink's permission.
It seems drink by drink alone is healed.

We drink them. We order and grow old
in taverns named for dire conditions.

Good Morning

Fifty-some years after the war, a kamikaze lands in my yard,
gently, like a sheet of newsprint.

"Ohayo gozaimasu," I say, though it is evening, light grown ochre
and pink, day disappearing across the Zero's wings.

He shinnies from the cockpit, the thinnest man I've seen.
He has evaded the radar. He's fallen

for decades, believing he'll attack
the coast of America, setting all the pines in Oregon blazing.

I take him inside, where he drinks a glass of water.
It is clear. It tastes nothing like the ocean.

God's Job

I surface in an office,
answering phones under false name. To keep from sleeping,

I wear contact lenses of transparent pornographic photographs
so I see my coworkers in the light of minglings

as if they floated in a palimpsest of their first history.
For fear of being pink-slipped, I do not exclaim, "No wonder.

They're someone's pleasure and someone's suffering."
In one pocket: a miniature of this city. In the other: a brick.

I alphabetize the file drawers labeled *Desires* and *Fears*.
The false name? I'm sworn to secrecy.

Matter

Matter goes by its many aliases: pine tree, match stick, missile whistling
increasingly distant from its silo and signal. All over America,

someone puts 40 cents of gasoline into a 15-year-old car, has beer and peanut butter,
sleeps in an arm chair outside her room in a work release motel north of town,

wakes on heating grates, wonders how the flower knows what shape to take,
watches the scrambled pornographic channel, prays hard. Only, scattered

on the land, fire, that natural redhead, is and acts, undoes the field mice
and grasses, makes the old book's pages frailer. We must turn them carefully.

If I Had Another Face

> *If I had another face, do you think I would wear this one?*
> —Lincoln-Douglas Debates
> *Abe Lincoln Was the Father of Professional Wrestling!*
> —Weekly World News

1.
Once, as a young man, Abe Lincoln choked on a cherry stone.
His eyes grew bigger. His face turned colors.
Abe Lincoln clutched his own throat, tilted over the dropped axe
whose handle pointed to the stand of trees
where the wood he'd been splitting bloomed.
A crow crossed over. It was noon.

2.
Abe Lincoln chortles at the joke he's told
to the mother of a boy who's died in the war
come two days by horse to visit him.
He touches his forehead, catches his breath,
repeats the punch line, "A fly in the butter churn. A fly."

3.
Leaves pitch in a fit of wind.
It's uncommonly sunny.
Some rise from piles.
Some just now falling are caught in the currents.
Abe Lincoln watches them.
They will not arrange themselves this way again.

4.
A masked Abe Lincoln prowls the ring.

Grammar

As if no language existed beyond that transmitted via drive-through window
 speakers
and we were forced to build from these few words the names of items for purchase

and their prices a lexicon and grammar capable of conveyance so conjuring
pity, fright, and longing ensued in listeners, yet so clear one could warn

of open manholes and rabid, racing animals, all purposes served, communication
largely a matter of context, duration, and inflection, in what setting and pauses

and stresses where transforming, "Can I get you anything else today" from "I envy
you your good fortune" to "This conversation has grown wearisome,"

"Here's your drinks" from "Not a cloud" to "Cancer," cents and dollars
Dewey-decimaled, so one amount refers to body parts, another to a movie star,

I mean it when I say, "Have a nice day. Drive on through. What kind of sauce?"
Say I name my moods, as if I might thus tame them, assign them codes like chess
 moves,

call the one I'm in "Dusk Sky over Berlin," "Stampede" the one I'm slouching to,
"Deliverance of the Angels" when I kiss you, when we bicker "Shooter on the
 Roof,"

with my weird Eden Adamed, indexed, might I then whistle my moods home
like animals, call their names and be stricken with them, pills that take hold

when commanded and always give; wasn't it this way for the first man: all
 phenomena
passed-out flesh some color returns to when called by the most plausible sounds,

yet left a little diminished, steaming water after frost-bite, worst cure
long-term, but the first, most comforting thought, or did the words aggrandize,

make more of the much and little already there, or, like slow and lukewarm
water, did they restore, return, as only you can, sensation in its terrifying measures?

And Then

Often I'm afraid a missile an anvil a bank safe will descend

pow on my head smackdab on the bald spot right through the circle it's said

the chakra the soul ascends and sets out on its rounds then my brain pan

soft pallet undoing all those dentists' labor shuttling through my thorax

and torso stomach splashing last night's wine and hummus

it happens in cities New York Chicago plummeting scaffolding and cornices

or my sad-sack dumb fuck cousin last I saw him small boy

at the funeral just before that the deathbed making fish lips like our grandfather's

dentureless gasping mouth then smacked in the face by my uncle

his father who saw me scowl then 21 two months out of prison breaking

and entering he claimed innocence of on the West side buying drugs

just smoke his friend in the car told police led down an alley and then

Alias

I'm the state enemy absent in the photographs
employees retouch, replaced with scenery:
extra steps to the lectern

where the famous mouth holds forth, the feared arms
gesture, the reproduction oil painting
in my children's children's classrooms.

I'm the quality of light expunged from lenses,
face that never struck a retina through glass,
altering a film of chemicals.

I'm the one on coins and stamps
if a currency commemorates the shadow
and the potted plant, in that country where a park's

named for me: *Slit With Razors From the Negatives*.
And in that park the statue honoring me
stands life-size: the censor's expert hands.

Shanty

Shame I can't treasure my skeleton,
prop it and toss glitter on it,
lift it and dance around with it.

Shucks that I can't show it off,
each bone there's a name for,
my expensive acquisition.

I'd pose it in positions,
Washington crossing the Delaware,
Mussolini head-tilt,

with scraps of newsprint in the eye sockets
and rags in the cranium.
A red paper heart to hang in the rib cage.

Gosh-darn that I can't see it outside of me,
my lily-white hinges, ankles,
and scary bare knuckles.

I'd hoist it off the front porch
in high winds, unnerve
neighbors when it clatters.

My Sentimental Education

Who poked Bazooka Joe's lost eye, what jape
was his gang engaged in, what joke
gone wrong, involving explosives

beer bottles were stolen
from their sleeping fathers for?
Maybe Bazooka caught a rusty nail

looking under the rug to see the floor show.
Maybe he stared and stared
through the wrong keyhole.

We'll never know. They never say
what happened to Joe. The eye patch is given.
All else is joking. Such lives,

they have to laugh though, and hard,
knocked twenty degrees backwards
a foot off the ground

every punch line, stunned into shooting
lines out their heads, black lines that float
like flattened haloes. It's a means of survival

for Bazooka and his gang, being poor, but proud,
with one set of clothes. Bazooka's always grinning
in his blue ball cap. Bazooka's always dumbfounding

the adults into stupor, and so never has to
go to sleep, mismatched pajamas and dirty sheets,
yanking the knotted shoelace down,

then walk across his small room so
tiptoed his ankles hurt, lying there in bed just
a skinny kid with one eye gone.

Cleaning

That's my face gaping in the hygienist's goggles, extra-simian,
eyes wide as a lab animal's, my mouth's blood on her surgical gloves.
She's all business, grim.

She scrapes the part of me most skeletal
so fiercely with instruments my ribs flinch.
It's all negligence and damage where those tiny harpoons land,

but who knew nerve ends meant this
blatancy, this weird, shimmery flutter in the chest?
Horizontal in the chair, I could be an autopsy,

may already occupy the fabled grave, except I see her,
my tongue all thumbs on the back of the mirror, and hear
country-and-western Muzak meant to soothe, or maybe that's the proof

I'm out of body, headed to some worse earth.
In the window above the dentist's stuffed bass, a hairy wrist
wipes a wet rag. The head that governs it looks in at me and grins.

$500,000 Policy

Spend every cent on my final expenses:
fireworks and rock bands, one fur-lined coffin

for each card in my wallet, truckloads of snacks:
nacho chips and Chuckles, your Ring Dings and Corn Nuts.

Tattoo labels on my eyelids, one per:
Never Better or *Miss You*. Outline the skeleton

along my skin with black-light ink, Latin names
in cursive script. Finance a student film

of my libretto, contralto, from beyond the grave,
beyond the range of human hearing, twenty-four hours

of "Race car, race car, race car" backwards fast.
Fly a TV-special magician and whatever assistants

right here. Hire them at any cost to cut me in half
for real and make those pieces disappear.

What Profits a Man

My press-on stigmata wow you more than my prescience,
re: where the face of Jesus will surface next: bearded and grinning
on each tortilla hand-flattened by Mrs. R. of Austin, Texas,
then fried in the fat that sketches and fills in his features,

every one a replica, so we mail-order and eat them, heated,
or so sorrowful and pained in the plate-glass smudges reappearing
next morning, no matter what cleaner, at the Alhambra Discount Theater,
address undisclosed, but near the ticket window, as the movie credits

roll, slow, and their letters rearrange, spell prayers and verses
ticket-holders utter. Watch for helicopters, television coverage,
box office boom. A woman sleeping with her children under cardboard
and an asphalt bridge awakes in leaky rain. Her looking makes a mirror

of a puddle and her eyes grow suddenly blue and bigger, like the paintings.
"God damn," she says, "God damn, God damn, God damn."
Her name's Arlene. Just ask her. The weeks-old sheets
of newsprint animated by a wind, their photographs now moving pictures,

broadcast a film on fences: documents the president secretly signed,
who the mayor had killed, which knife your neighbor
held to her throat, what all the children ate. There's my ad: Press-On Stigmata,
4 for $10. I seem to be bleeding. I drip. My wounds look convincing

Scenes

Against the lingerie-color sunset,

orange and pink and filmy as a negligee, two dogs fight in a liquor store parking lot, mouths on throats, blood an inkling in the neon advertising bargains on imports. Their long shadows go slo-mo in the skittering gravel and spin under dust's little weather systems. Customers seem to glow, sidling past then leaving with purchases.

Even the curtains move

woozily in a room the knockout gas has seeped through, making the rug and the lampshade and the couch smell like medicine. A man whistles and tilts, does a dance called "My Whole Body Feels Like an Arm I've Slept Funny On." He believes he's an iceberg. He thinks he's a thundercloud. Suddenly he sings, "Oh, I could die right here, in the delirium of air."

Footprints in a prison yard's snow,

different sizes of the same shoe in loopy, raggedy patterns, fill with those drifting hieroglyphs falling a long way to shine all night in the floodlights. They scroll in horizontal lines like a stream of arbitrary numbers. Snow fills the nest a bird has built bit by bit by bit (burnt matches, newsprint, hair) in the fence's concertina wire.

Rags soaked in so much fuel

the basement boiler seen past them looks shimmery catch fire. How leisurely flames stroll unfinished wallboards. Through attic windows, angled daylight, speckled with dust, shines on a dictionary with pages stained yellow, orange, and purple with pressed summer wildflowers.

The antique pornographic film

projected across a kneeling man's unclothed back, bodies doing what along his spine, stays nothing more than light that might well ceaselessly travel, swift and immaterial, when he rises and steps aside, but here someone's sudden, outstretched palm lifts in front of the rays: two torsos splayed out on the fingers and sepia splashing gallery walls.

Who is it holds film

up to sunlight beside a parked car in a desert, squinting through each frame threaded between her thumb and forefinger? The engine ticks, and a few lizards flit from cactus to cactus, making time seem to stutter. She stands in a long, flowered dress, seeing far purple hills with one eye and something that makes the expression on her face change and change and change with the other.

Dusk, shadows

grown long on the freshly cut public park grasses, the few children not called home yet run faster from swings to slides and back again. The many-colored lights of televisions sparkle through house windows all around. One small boy hears his mother then lies down and plays dead, level with the lit horizon and bigger than the distant, scribbled mountains.

Ceiling fans burn

drinkers' cigarettes quicker, adrift in ashtrays, held dreaming between fingers, pressed trembling to lips. One woman shakes hers toward her listener, punctuating points she makes, their faces softened in the long, wavery mirror. One hour, the drink special's over, but who can tell the time in here? The clock between two vodka bottles runs, what, 15, 20, 30 minutes faster?

Noon, a woman

walks from her front door to the mountains, through foothills, where trees run to scrub, then, higher, to aspen. Air thins, and she stops to rest, imagining the purely skeletal repeated figure journeying in scrolls: one person at separate times and increased heights. She stands near a pool of water at the summit in barely enough light to see the house she's traveled far from.

A man puts his hand

on his wife's face as they sleep. She presses her wrist to the back of his neck. All night they coil and wreathe like the letters of the alphabet of a language whose last native speaker died long ago, their blankets, kicked away and pulled back again, writing and erasing them. After the alarm clock, she moves to say something. He puts a finger to her lips.

Hair waving like lake grasses

fish flicker through—a body standing upright under water seems a body in a larger, larger room—arms held up and forward like a sleepwalker's, who leaves the house in nightclothes to drift through a meadow, head tilted skyward as if searching a ceiling for cracks. Wound around the legs, rope's woven through the cinder blocks it takes to anchor this one, who sways like someone hearing distant, beautiful music.

The body,

surface area inches above the water's, rises and slides over the lip of a claw-footed bathtub, around which floorboards, beneath their checkerboard linoleum, weaken and leak. Single drops spatter a bare carpet downstairs. The body's fall shakes a few photographs from a table. They, too, climb, a few, like the body, face up. On the water's level, ascending finish, the letters of an inked note run.

Buildings, people,

street-level neon gleam in the moving mirror a bus window makes in a sunlit city. How much eyes must see in each filmed frame: drinkers through a bar's open doorway, one shoe on a sidewalk, scattering pigeons, and they beaks, heads, fat bodies lifted on oily wings. *Checks Cashed*, *Bail Bonds*, *Good Food*, *Tattoo* flash, letters backwards, across a passenger's sleeping face.

Gulf Coast

"Heck," I said, hallucinogenic in Texas City, Texas,
a whistle stop like many days without sleep, the vapory, striated air

combustible and wobbly, the sheen of refined fuel dizzying.
God knows what awfulness-on-the-earth all-told

the colossal, flaring lean-tos on the edge of town were home to.
We ate fried oysters and cole slaw. Our glasses of beer stood yay tall.

Passersby in the windowpane wore expressions
like those on the faces in abnormal psychology texts,

eyes blackened for anonymity but not reprieve from their distress.
They walked around as if undressed.

We sat undermined by substances. The tape loop of my blood
spun. I saw through my closed eyelids

afterimages of Heimlich charts, opened them and read
a government-issue poster: *WHAT TO DO IN CASE OF CHEMICAL*

interrupted by her pale, halter-topped bare shoulder,
in which I more sensed than saw the entourage of atoms

shimmying on their hinges. Some outsized cloud of toxic gases
any moment might have risen like a drastic jellyfish.

I said, "Heck." We paid the bill and took our chances. Many
ambulances hurried through the sun's last, almost acrobatic light. At the motel,

atoms did their rope tricks. Hands and knees in the bathroom, eyes
inches from the tile, I whispered, "Look here."

Lay My Burden Down

Anstett, scofflaw, drives valid licenseless
through the rural *mise-en-scene*, sun
relentless at the extremity of its sweep.

With encyclopedic command of penny-ante illegality,
Anstett, criminally jockeying his standard transmission
one mile an hour under posted limits,

goes uncaught, to and from his latest stint.
Oh, he rakes it in in the world's perpetual elegy
for each prior instant. Anstett has convictions

it all ends in tears. Ask him as he jaunts hungover by
a cow struggling to stand on sheet ice in a pasture,
legs ridiculously splayed and stunningly unperpendicular.

He knows where the damage that used to be animals
has been done by all things vehicular.
When he gets to work, he starts drafting memoranda.

What does Anstett wear
through all this illicitness, motion, and grief?
Wingtips, shirt, and tie. Fridays office casual.

Life and Death at the DMV

What auspice is this, face crazed
in the photograph I take everywhere as evidence

I'm allowed, bearing the exact expression I'll wear
pulled over for something serious, negligence

laws'll be invented for? I'm one insolent
expletive, all appearances, one dangerous motorist.

I'm driving down the sidewalk backwards drunk,
raising livestock within city limits in the duct-taped trunk,

negotiating turns while reading pornography,
watching the wounded grow small and smaller in front of me.

Work

Orange trees swayed. A family ate sandwiches
wrapped in newspaper they did not know one word of.
The father scolded the smallest daughter
to put her shirt on, though her breasts had not yet begun.
He hated the mark on her shoulder where the burlap bag had hung.

Declarative

Some children have caught a small animal.
Birds move jerkily, like early motion photography.
We wait downriver, as if for a child in swathing.
She takes a hallucinogen and sees people pursued by skeletons.
Her canvases come to resemble slaughterhouse workers' clothing.

A man boards a bus with a torso in his carry-on.
The television news anchor's wrists are tied with coat hangers.
The formula spans several chalkboards and carries tremendous implications.
Something has made the swans ill; they vomit by the rowboats.
A scuffle on the barge draws a crowd.

Explosive devices lie dormant in the emptied building.
The clock's glass face grows hairline fractures.
A man in the town square talks loudly.
A woman quickly gathers her belongings.
The shop owner unlocks the door.

Holes in the Story

1.
If physics allowed actual cartoon thought balloons,
you'd see I'm again daydreaming of miniature hot air balloons
adrift about living rooms and you
heroin smuggled in stomachs
whose acids dissolve rubber and poison balloons
bloodstreams, souls ascending from bodies like balloons.

2.
Like souls in bodies, air inside balloons remains invisible,
film not yet rinsed in chemicals.
Our ancestors' spidery handwriting grows invisible
on frail and frailer pages going see-through.

3.
Sometimes foreseeing blurry, weeping faces,
I grimace in mirrors for practice,
sober and stoic in those merciless surfaces
like a man I might be one day, who faces
hard news with courage while all around him faces
go watery and he sees souls flicker in voices, faces.

Satellites

That's us in the satellite photographs,
in flagrante delicto through the atmosphere.

You can tell by the tattoos: starfish ashore on your ankle,
daggered Ace of Spades bloodless on my shoulder blade.

You're pressing your knuckles to my vestigial tailbone.
I'm saying something urgent to your jugular vein.

See: that pile's what we wore that day: your mismatched lingerie,
my NASA boxer shorts and T-shirt with wine stains.

It seems, at least, we've bathed, but the soles of my feet
shine with calluses. Your toenail polish has flaked.

Thank gravy we're not wearing outfits, or, heavens,
playing Prison Escape. By the sunlight on our bodies,

it's neither early nor late. Something shadows my face.
Your eyes are closed. You've made a cradle of your legs.

Winter

At closing time in Davenport, two women kissed fiercely,
as if making some refusal in the terrifying light

suddenly cast across all our faces
and tabletops and plastic cups

of various quantities and conditions of liquid
the law allowed us little time to finish drinking.

I didn't have to go home, but I couldn't stay there.
Bars were still serving across the river.

I read all the notices against fighting and bad checks
and an article about the regular beaten to death

taped to a mirror bearing the bar's name and logo.
Bottles doubled there in image but not content,

then the women, pressed against each other's jackets.
Each had her eyes closed. I cannot know

what it was for them their mouths meant.
One held the other's head as if to steady it.

Prayer Against Dying on Camera

Lord, not shot in liquor store stick-up,
jugular uncorked and finely misting or

splatter-patterning display case plate glass
and me so many pixels collapsing

at the feet of bikini'd cardboard
cutout models, purchase a puddle,

last words of my kind, "Oh, shit,"
lip-readable. Jesus not suddenly

in latex novelty emporium or slam-
bang stroke on jumbotron in a coliseum

screaming, not tumbling
from the burning building in a series

of photographs, speed increasing,
one frame famous because I look so calm.

Prayer for Safe Travel

God bless cars with red cellophane tape over brake lights,
padlocks for trunk locks, different color doors, lumber for bumpers,

windshields zigzag fractals those who outlive lightning wear
everywhere under skin, nearly insignia, tributary maps.

Keep them distant from auto impound's concertina wire,
corkscrewed as cartoon pigs' tails or paper streamers from exploding

party favors. Leave their drivers untroubled. When we follow
open-frame trucks with several green, missile-size bottles

upright and wobbling, extinguish our cigarettes, dispel all fear
and static electricity. Let us clearly see the diamond-shaped flammable

symbol, its twist of white lines a burning-bush flicker, its number
3 religious, as promise to spare us while climbing

hills behind dump trucks of jostling rubble and rebar
or vehicle carriers stacked with those spectacular wrecks.

Ardor

When I've traveled somewhere so distant I cannot help her,
my very hands buried, or lost, or ash,
when I've come to the world no one returns from,
may my daughter have grown yet more brave and whip-smart

in this one, tall and mouthy, even, eyes far-flung
and beguiling. I would bestow on her the power
to hypnotize landlords and bosses, thugs and policemen,
to pay for all purchases with her singular smile

and return grief to its source. Failing that, I wish her routine
troubles only. Sweet Jesus, nothing outlandish:
her parents' deaths before hers as she approaches her dotage,
one toothache for practice, one flat tire for measure.

May her exaltations be often. May she love whom she loves
with ferocity and hate what she does with equal ardor.
May she believe what I once believed, but longer,
each minute a kingdom, and she the strongest vying sovereign.

Answer

For which you'll study the debris-strewn intersections
and stricken faces your remaining days, may they lengthen,
as if some grain of disaster still hovered there,

and you, having isolated it, work at an antidote.
Guesses you hazard: capsule of powdered glass, treatment plan
by which squad lights widen irises, and everything seen

through them thereafter shines. In this shimmer,
you develop your theorem of a fixed measure
of suffering, that there is now no more or less torment

than was or will be, but it wanders. Here a woman
is hurt with pliers. Here the killer watches a comedy.
You call it *No Accident*, and it sustains you,

even thrown through a windshield, stones in your mouth,
even when you drift, combing each tatter of newsprint for what?
Winning numbers? The blazing script of your own name?

You glimpse it in footprints, whatever direction, in road signs
and outdoor advertisements, especially in the eyes of animals
frightened at night: the startling liquid that washes us

ceaselessly, grasses springing back at each step.
Something, you know, is not forthcoming. Something,
like God, is everywhere but hidden, like skin under clothes.

From *Each Place the Body's* (2007)

Trouble

> *The sleepers are very beautiful as they lie unclothed.*
> —Whitman

If we trouble each sleeper, house to house and room by room,
ditches to hotel beds, propping our lit lamps

to their sudden, jack-o-lanterned expressions, and ask
who burnt insects with sun and a magnifying glass,

how many glasses of water in that fast-moving cloud,
what is it sloshes inside us like iced drinks on the boat's deck

as some intermittent music, wind chimes or sirens,
drifts from the floating casino ablaze as the candelabrum

of nerve ends in the wakened sleeper's fist, if we ask
what of it if it got wet instead of dark at night, not damp,

but gallons, and it's happening, in Fiji and Nebraska, quiz
which they'd be then: millionaire or tugboat captain,

gracious bingo champ or rope company rep, please clarify
your answers, we should nearly whisper so as not to rouse them.

Undressed

We get undressed, uncivilize ourselves,
and while the television programming

and sicknesses of animals do not cease,
we reach such a pitch we're purely body,

beyond its umpteen miseries,
enduring uproar in our skins so keen

it cannot be rendered, what we *a capella* say
all vowel and glottal stop. Is that your face

and these I grasp your only feet?
This dizzy, how can I wear a tie,

looking serious in shoes to feed a parking meter?
How is it we're citizens, some day die,

and ape that ache and release here, eyes jittering
blunt and slit? Geometry claims an infinity

of instances, or nearly, cook up a surface.
Example: yours, bewildering my nerve ends,

putting the nuance into nuisance,
apple to apocalypse, in this brief kingdom

where God and the devil call truce, lie down
like dogs who fight each other but are exhausted.

Redolence

The names of things are always guesses, sometimes gorgeous,
a single instance taken to excess.

Air's fluent through the grasses
some feet above the usual bones
of many languages' last native speakers.

They're out of common parlance.
They're any utterance's antithesis.

When my daughter speaks, each word's approximation,
The way the days seem, each an increasingly nearer version.

What words should a person say, waking penniless and drunk,
with no hope of not sobering, sick, the day plain,
the edge of each thing clear in sun, of which every fire on earth

is redolent, the one at the heart of things and here in a cigarette?

Country

A man asleep in his work clothes
shall not be lifted bodily

to float like lit and falling newsprint
and wake in flames as a voice commands him.

A headline won't print that morning
across his vision, telling him how to live.

A luminous ampersand does not tattoo
itself on his sternum, joining everything,

spinning landscape that extends
from the fingers of each hand

when he turns to find some matches,
all he can see and farther

as he smokes the day's first cigarette.
His name's stitched over five shirt pockets,

four clean ones and the one he slept in.
He wears it now, lifting each fifth part

to his eyes for inspection: cracks
and misprints. Some grand blueprint

does not emerge on a napkin
from the parking lot lunch cart.

His burrito's the same as ever,
hot above the asphalt.

His children sit in a classroom
he sat in. The teacher spins the globe

and stops it with her longest finger.
She's picking the country where someone lives.

Storefronts

1.
That daylight should be daylight so utterly
as, in the ten-million storefronts of my country,
clerks adjust the latest fashions on mannequins,
and here illegals wear boards on their knees
to level concrete outside an investment firm's offices,
volcanic, curdled earth, at the entrance
of the building from which I nightly am disgorged

2.
means the memoranda of America insist
chronic tardiness will jeopardize your position on the a.m. shift,

3.
but maybe we're living in a demonstration model home,
light through the skylight fetched in by light bulb.
Maybe every day's Saturday. Maybe it's Sunday.
A recording somewhere plays the cough
of a dog's bark and friends in the next room.
Maybe it's play food in the unplugged refrigerator

4.
in my country, where the water tastes like somebody's mouth,
where I can't keep count of what I'm angry at
and lie down like any animal, in some dark place to sleep.

Reinventing the Wheel

Begin with liquid: tiny wagon wheels of tap water,

miniature bicycle tires of blood for lice to ride on,

lawn mowers floating over circles of rose-

petal wine, a pocket watch's glittery gears

fashioned from dew. Make hoops of the gases:

race car tires concocted entirely of oxygen,

village children chasing smoke rings with sticks.

Self-Portrait in Corporate Offices

Anstett glances, attempting his best alert, intelligent animal look,
interested in project schedules, imagines being taxidermied, pelt propped
up with sawdust and armature, remembers Duchamp's *In Advance*

of the Broken Arm snow shovel and once, skull a hovel, apocalyptic
squalor of red wine hangover, listing least painful ways. Who'd he
eat first, surviving plane crash? With whom repopulate the earth,

world's end? Anstett switches tack, scribbles repeatedly in the margins
of a project plan, "Lord, make me your. . .," then whispers thanks
to the atoms of his face, loyal to just one brand of bad luck.

Needling

1.
In our bodies, we move uniformly.
No one owns a rickshaw tattoo
that actually clatters, hip to rib,
dust rising off the skin.

2.
Across my torso,
print a flesh-tone color tattoo
of the word *Invisibility*.

3.
Think of people
with their own names emblazoned
as if they might forget.
Call me anything:
alphabet braceleting one wrist.

4.
Circling an ankle: many nations' monuments.
She stepped from the bath like a giantess.

5.
An old man's arm tattoos,
green like just-before tornadoes
and the taste of anesthesia.
Once, nothing shone so brightly for him.

6.
Tattoo two lungs
and I'll return yearly
to have them darkened.

7.
How bare the body looks
around the first one.

8.
Best, for me, the flaming prophecies:
Stick Knife Here, *Born to Die*,
the ones redundant at autopsies:
stream of air bubbles
rising from the mermaid's red mouth
on a drowned man's palm.

Prayer for Recompense

Snowballs iceballs, I demand to be paid here on in with oversize prize checks,
my name silvery and glittering, surface area and dollar amounts so large

I bungee-cord lash them to each week's brand-new roof rack, manhandle
monetary instruments drive-through window huge, lift across bank parking lots,

spun this way and that in the trillionaire wind. Jaw-droppingly rich,
the children construct lean-tos and rafts, kites rising miles,

or luge and toboggan, ink a precious-metal sheen smearing wintry hills.

Blessings

Distance makes the stars pristine. Near, they'd savage seeing,
weird trick, seance eyes and the mind hold. Here, they're prim,

as if one by one arranged. There, the annihilating
heat and light, so absolute they are each other, prove something

enraged grants mercy, does not destroy us utterly, as Greek gods
were said to do. Murderous plural, in what larger struggle

do stars exhaust themselves, and how could the soul,
that insubstantial, be anything but swift, but where to,

leaving a body set on seeing in stark, colossal ovens?
I sit with my daughter on the front steps, counting them.

"One, two, three, four, five," she says.

Proposition

Is it so wrong to love my voting booth, our privacy and quiet
when I turn my back to the precinct officials, step in,
pull the little curtain, and, with a stylus, make my desires clear?
Is it wrong to love the language of ballot initiatives,
how they make even "shall" and "levied" sound sexy,
wrong loving my own name in the rolls to show I'm permitted,
there with my address like a magazine subscription or blood donation label?
Yes or no, shall I be shunned for wishing
through a window in the back of each booth stands a candidate
and I kiss them and make my decision?

Simple

The gunman hovers on closed-circuit camera,
x-number of ones and zeroes,
face flushed pinker, if this were color.

Signs boast bargains in liquor.
He says something quickly, the visible
part of his mouth growing smaller and bigger.

The weapon's spectral, glints
where he holds it far from him
like a rare and dangerous mineral.

The time and date blink.
Behind the clerk,
little, illegible bottles burst.

Flight

Swallowed condoms plump with cocaine rupture,
split like too-ripe fruit and spill their cargo,
washing ferrying passengers' stomachs,

followed down with little whiskey bottles,
lit by windowed sunset, emptied into
splashing plastic tumblers. Shades drawn, each eye's

iris widens. Nerve ends hallelujah
over checker-boarded fields. People
go to sleep or listen to their neighbors
sigh. Some others, accidentally sickened,

die before the EMTs arrive, or,
no, before the planes descend to asphalt,
slow, and rest at last like sleepers breathing
quietly, quietly, quietly, hushed.

Burglars

Cameras small as aspirin capsules,
smaller, each lens a grain of medicine,
injected, ride illuminated veins,

slam-bang along then through those passages'
walls, orbiting rockets abruptly un-
hinged, photographing what-all a body

hides, as now a stubbed-toed burglar whispers
curses, hissing, though nobody's home.
Her see-through negligee drapes a chair. He's
tried it on, over his work clothes: wrong size.

Lied. I lied. No such cameras
whir through bloodstreams yet, and the burglar stripped
first, pale, scared, lingerie a perfect fit,
cried until his mirrored image blurred.

Glass Mingled with Fire

A sheet of newsprint ghosted by wind
blouses and billows in earliest light
each day down an alley, solitary,
air's only occupant at that hour, or
over the Jesus-loved heads of sleepers
on sidewalks, whispery pages
heralding latest savings.

The creek of my childhood flooded,
rinsed abandoned newspaper boxes,
fish small headlines glass cracks
magnified, coin boxes jimmied, refuse
left evidence, past poor houses,
vehicles, as quarry water bore
trespassers mercifully mostly.

Tabernacle

Birds' random
shadow patterns,

dusk, on vandalized,
sun-bleached

panels of abandoned
drive-in screens,

melancholy in daylight,
lot a clearing

in the cornfields
or sand,

and speaker-boxes,
some not yet baseball-

batted, on duplicate
poles staggered

like national
cemetery markers,

as quiet, but what
music and moaning

once, the deepest
secrets, fiercest

screams, whisperings,
how many children

in pajamas racing
through gravel

a light rain
now valorizes,

as if on cue,
by stagecraft?

Where are the films
of yesteryear,

"film" for that thin veneer
where light stopped

disappearing, rushing
its distances,

to splash, lavish,
Pompeian lava,

the still
of a sudden animate

with what maniacal
octopi, car crashes?

Indeed I Was

Skinny then, little more than skeleton,
naked next to an actual skeleton,

my *memento mori* 3-D X-ray. The professor lifted
each bare limb, then made me mimic the skeleton's

positions, asking the anatomy art class to see
the bones in my skin matched the skeleton's

poses. Easy to see so early and cold
on plywood stage in a studio how soon I'd be a skeleton,

what little dress of hair-on-end flesh above tibia and ulna,
cranium, mandible, fluorescents on the skeleton

and me merciless, and a square of skylight sun.
Charcoal and pencils scratched. I didn't ask, "Whose skeleton,"

or exclaim, "Alas, poor _____,"
the palm of my hand open like the skeleton's,

eyes above easels everywhere, clothed legs below.
On their sketch pads I imagined me and the skeleton

synchronized: *tai chi*, Rockettes, country line-dancing,
me on a bar floor, skeleton

kicking my undressed ribs. "Now, Mr. Anstett,"
Professor Something said, "if you could embrace the skeleton . . ."

Appetite

Resurrected, resuscitated zombie Elvis Presley
karate-chops through Graceland's solid-core doors,

insane for car keys, then brains, then sandwiches,
but cannot drive fast enough to bask in each gleam

of vanishing sunlight, purple and black and pink
as lingerie each number of miles, so unbolts the Lisa Marie,

anchored in asphalt, hot-wires, siphons jet fuel,
and flies, humming the early tunes, acoustic,

from the 1968 comeback special, thinned down
and joking with all the back-up singers,

The Blossoms this time,
not The Jordanaires.

Each Day

When my soul escapes from my body, I chase it, looking foolish
as a man running after his hat with no head on his torso, or
a small boy at the carnival pursuing released balloons when his arms
sheared off in the tilt-a-whirl's gears, blood festooning all over.

A headline rises from its story, floats like skyline fractions of something
above horizon, no matter the continent or people afflicted.
Classifieds advertise all manner of bargains:
Wedding dress, unworn. Child's crib, never used.

But I catch my soul, in fingertips, each hand, like a leaf shivering
down in wind, tip-toe on window ledge so many stories up
birds dizzy. No helping any thread or grain of wood.
Sorry, friends. It flutters. Shining. Symbolic.

Free Beer Tomorrow

In the tavern, surly parolees
recall cellies, rock-paper-scissor
who buys next, countertop before them
crime-scene diorama: full shot glass
liquor store, matchbook getaway car,

ashtray lake to hide the evidence.
Future or past tense I cannot catch
straining, perched only two stools over,
over the jukebox's long, warbling
litany of loss and regret, wrongs

and squandered love, eerie steel-pedal
elegies, ancient lamentations,
and the pocket calls, clatter and smack,
and couples arguing who's drunker
and safe to drive home, and bartender

yelling "Last call," everyone buying
fervently the biggest drinks at once.
Maybe I misheard. I dare not ask
to start my new life now, ride along
as lookout, begin my criminal

apprenticeship observing, rise up
through attrition, and then mastermind.
Lit as I am, how could I describe
these three to police on the payphone
there by the bathrooms, *HIS* and *HERS* clear?

And probably I have it all wrong:
orchestra of bottles, church organ
pipes, doubles in the mirror, meaning
possibility, many-color
innards all sorts of bright exit signs.

Their gesture of sliding the matches
flat around a whiskey glass may mean
instead the ballet of the self toward
the other and how the two only
ever asymptotically glance,

longing a series of near-misses.
Reading the sign *FREE BEER TOMORROW*,
I might be the man I imagine
misunderstands, rising each morning
thereafter hoping, who'll gladly pay

for those sad songs, pickled eggs ghostly
in medical exhibit water,
but demands free beer, just one, pounding
early, shouting, "Open up. Open
the door. It's tomorrow already!"

From *Insofar as Heretofore* (2014)

Atoms in Their Orbits

The particulars of remembering, spray
of water beyond the singularity of its gravity-
defying thrust, color of carpet hairs

under fingernails, or screech of laughter
one hotel hallway at an ice machine's
languid rumbling, or the house of my childhood

haunted by what menace, mysterious
injuries. Gingerly, the wind, with hints
of vanilla, tobacco, wet stone, continues

over whatever Texas road down which a thin
dog falters, brothel, your skin,
public wall on which hand-scrawled messages appear,

grass seldom slept on well or long, skeleton
in the mountains after the thaw, glass
shattered on asphalt, many glittering windows.

Self-Portrait as Jackass on Dash Cam

Unclear officer or offender,
pixilated on basic cable,
blurred, limbs whirringly,
windmillingly obscured,
turbulent in landscape

of squad car windshield frame,
Yosemite Sam angry,
hopping foot to foot
in whiskey-lacquered jig,
hollering, "Consarn it, unhand

the schoolmarm, varmint!,"
Jesus-at-Gethsemane-
looming-crucifixion-stewed,
stutteringly Barney Fife flummoxed,
sputteringly preposterous,

flustered it seems by every substance,
wrathy impresario of cussedness,
engaged in solo cage match brawl,
raging harangue,
epileptically apoplectic,

dyspeptic, itinerant fiasco,
spectacular, tantruming fracas,
semaphore-signaling without flags,
seemingly summoning so many
non-responding rescue craft.

Errors and Omissions

I lose faith in object persistence listening in murk to physicist
narrate creation, loping from podium to laser-point
PowerPoint to pinpoint main point: initial burst of pith,
whooshing jot to oodles, fleck to superfluity of viscera,
scintilla's blurt and splurge, peripatetic incipience sashay
before, my lights, topic proper: exact replica of auditorium
down to expressions on faces in photos in wallets, text
histories on cell phones, same toes poking through stockings,
verbatim fray on plum blouse hem, me remembering bottle
of ketchup slid too fast and splashing, only this glitch:
universe +1, my name on license Puritan version:
Increase Anger; universe +2, oracular: *Early Grave*.
Another, son sitting with me daughter, this poem better,
or identical genders and names but atmosphere a curdled
pousse café of grain alcohol and meringue. Then I insist,
in infinite infinities, each its hitch, for whatever I suppose
the soul the tinge and gist, even infinitesimal, of permanence.

All at Once

In the beginning was the whir. The whir made flecks.
Impossible now a snow across the roads like smoke, animated lace, supple, hovering tracery. Impossible such tall flames.
Somewhere mutter every word we must not blurt in airports.
Somewhere hum to thrum of wind over bottle's lip.
Somewhere maneuver shopping cart, mouthing brand names.
Somewhere lurch and curse in barroom murk, clutching torn felt.
Somewhere say "Maple, loblolly," watching light dwindle through windows.
Somewhere tiptoe on stairs pressing bald spot to ceiling, making of it sombrero's brim.
Whereof one cannot speak, thereof one must be silent.
The world is all that just decays.

Bluff as a Theorem

> *Indeed, this world is flat; as for the other, nonsense.*
> —Jules Laforgue

My blood girds up, and that knucklehead, my heart,
says its two words over and over. This filibuster
of dark and light and dark again just doesn't stop.

Now I might swagger the front stoop, bluff
as a theorem, taking my empty hands for proof
the world's full, trees trembling all down the street,

birds steaming. Wind slugs through the heat, flattens
paper to the fences. Every window liquors up with sun.
Maybe I could stagger a sidewalk all day, scared

and mortal, lighting matches one by one.
Wouldn't I cower like I'd proven
the world truly flat, blood riding my veins like a bus route?

Coliseum

Mostly tedium:
Light, shadow
retreat, advance
across the dust's expanse.
Sparrows worry insects,
one limbless as an antique statue.

Manos 84.13.72

How many living hands have labored, worked
what humble instruments the labored work
of many hands to each day give us this,
whichever indexical, ravenous
us each day awakes? Stone a fashioned shape
suggests the shaping hands but more. The ground
the hands unearthed, the stones that struck the stone,
the wind that day or night or none, the stars
and moon and sun and how they were supposed.
"We need to eat," I think the first prayer goes,
but I'm American and ignorant,
each day amply fed. Plainly as I can,
in fingered meter, slapdash, awkward cant:
this stone stuns me, its color human skin.

Are Those Real Songs or Did You Write Them?

Ask who thinks it's easy
making a killing making
balloon animals shaped
like furniture and thoughts.

Shall we accept some
say of your libretto
crisp and stringent
except that muddle in the middle?

Let the poem just like the afternoon
be abruptly interrupted
with WOOF and echoing
smack of hammers,

splat of drops that taste
like us of dust and salt
and tests confirm convey
trace amounts of rain.

That Feeling of Impending Doom? Impending Doom.

Urgent, lurching, cyclone-chartreuse
cloud of household cleaner mismatch?

Whiff of catastrophe from beaker and flask?

Plummeting to enlarging ground that looms and looms?

The uh-oh of wanting and oh-no of having?

Descending grand piano's widening shadow?

So-and-so in throes of lousy mood?

Startling at dawn, feeling I'll die of who I am?

Silhouette in midnight farmhouse window?
Lantern light flickering as victim's here signal?

Bedside table, trial transcript bound in convicted's skin?
Killer rising fully clothed from river, grinning?

Graveyard lit by lightning?
Clown mask and surgical gown in glove box?

Carnival din—calliope, screaming—from somewhere ill-lit?
Abandoned asylum we're lured to?

Apex of arc
when object swerves
from rise to fall,
in that instant
neither at all?

Narrative Impulse

A character in a joke, the priest,
let's suppose, interrupts to tell a story
about how much rain inside rain
and coffee franchise so rampant
within each coffee drop exists
an infinitesimal but otherwise identical
functioning replica, endlessly. Sleepy,
he forgets to liken this to God's love.
Then the rabbi tells one about two drunks
sack-racing on the flattest road out of town,
each dreaming himself the hero.

Ample Evidence

Reading all autumn afternoon about deaths of philosophers

In quality of fiery and earth-toned light we might construe as rueful

Quarreling in mind with one definition of miracle

Thinking again about suffering and the ephemeral

Then how to speak eloquently of cat-piss carpet in cinderblock apartment

Overwhelmed by memory of mouth and brain overtaken by phenomena

Such as flesh of an apricot and other

Conceptions extending the realm of the possible

Confirming occurrence of appearance of the unthinkable

Like videotape of man levitating in air

Or becoming corpse, magician's last, best trick

Self-Portrait with Spoiler Alerts

In romantic comedy I must adhere
to wacky codicil in will
demanding astral levitation
and dating psychic phlebotomist.

"Hello, hello," I wave and yodel,
then wander farther yonder, calling,
"Pick me," direct dotted-line object
of the zombies' outstretched arms,
leading economic indicator scruffy fringes of their shirt cuffs.

I dream I watch Andy Warhol's *Sleep* in 3-D IMAX,
poet John Giorno snoozing giant for hours,
and wake festooned with popcorn, lap soaked with cola.

As if light were altered by what it touches,
dirtied by glancing on gutter water,
then traveled scattered, smudged,

I'm already nostalgic for what just happened,
endlessly reminiscent about each prior instant,
flickers on outskirts of vision,
those iffy, flimsy instances

ceaselessly expanding, factor by which flashback
content increases in each subsequent sequel.

Self-Portrait with Product Placement

I dreamed I taught a writing class and warned,
"Never start a poem 'I dreamed,'"
adding, "A perfect rhyme begins
Black Sabbath's 'War Pigs':

'Generals gathered in their masses
Just like witches at Black Masses,'"
both of which I've said in writing classes.
What bad advice and sleep-inducing dream life!

Next morning I wait for you in shopping mall bookstore,
faux-leather armchair, sit like goofball
listening to couple giggle in Erotica one aisle over
as I read and do not pay for retail theft *roman à clef*.

Tonight I'll dream I watch my face grow slacker
as I grow drunker drinking liquor,
features fun-housed in warped bar mirror,
brand-name secret pending contract.

Unresolved Conflict

I dreamed a pony with the face of Freud,
glasses just so, beard immaculate, chewed grass tufts,
dropping cigar ash, tail swatting behind in vivid sunset.

Foreshortened centaur, lacking human arms and neck and torso,
he made whinnying pronouncements I barely followed, my German rusty,
his munching fervent. My best guess:
America a mistake, a giant mistake, the clover *luscious*.

Against Interpretation of Dreams

I dreamed I watched my eyeballs flick
in unison below their lids

like muscles under a strong man's skin
or water over water something large swims

or twin sleepers beneath sheets
or a belly's waves of fetal limbs,

synchronized parallel rivulets
I tried no luck to interpret, like reckoning

plotline by watching faces watching film.
Dream me found it kind of cartoony

and creepy, then saw myself sleepwalk
about construction sites zombie-lurchy,

up and down see-sawing, barrel-fulcrumed
boards, arms out in air in front of me.

If the TV Will Not Be Used at All During the Entire Diary Survey, Indicate the Reason Below

- *TV is broken*
- *Everyone is away on vacation*
- *Other*
—Nielsen Viewing Diary

1. Suddenly utterly Amish.

2. Reception awful inside volcano.

3. Bracing for End of Days.

4. Out of ammo following Elvis freakout re-enactment.

5. Fear mind read.

6. Fear dying thoughts sitcom theme song, deathbed or alleyway, as spirit drifts toward light and/or flames frantic banjo and folksy nostrums.

7. *Real Depressives of Schenectady* cancelled.

8. Ditto *Man vs. Cattle*.

9. TV devil.

10. TV sees me.

Memorial

Say that near or distant day at least he died
doing what he most loved: meeting and exceeding
customer expectations. Until then, God's truth, I'll likely lie

around and name and name and name again each body part,
mostly old testament and smattering of presidents.
I must accept some day I'm praying hands and knees

in hospital hallway and/or stricken, hectoring slippery,
room-temperature rotisserie chicken wobbling on palm
like stage-prop skull or lonely as a cosmonaut, asleep

in clothes like Russian novel's drunkard. Because Jesus
called the mustard seed the smallest seed, I plot these precious
few hours to scour the world of smaller seeds, endeavor

outlandish as ploy of the American Acclimatization Society
to import every kind of bird in Shakespeare. No one calls
our Lord mistaken. Say this about me, as I was saying.

Care and Feeding

Some number—10,000?—scintilla swing like saloon doors,
invisibly hinged, upon and in this heat-blurred

landscape and who-poured ocean. Piñatas
my brain-shaped sway, one for each cell left.

As blindfolded batters gather, I forget
which firework my soul most longs for,

hearing disembodied conversation through wallboards,
but, good start, air condensed to water sweating down milk glass

as elsewhere cows' stomachs translate grasses,
and I greet the day as so often it is: as-is,

each wee hour dream my new career: obit punch-up,
collective noun creation: squalor of Anstetts,

bickering of in-laws, or assign myself such perilous missions
as searching glove boxes, trunks in impound lots for the unknown's

whereabouts and attendant engineering specs
to nth-level granularity and zoom-in view

and the vanishing point toward which, on what
so-and-so's say-so, the 10,000 things drift.

Progress

Today The Lumbering Shuffle.
Tomorrow Foam Rubber Donut, Awkward Glance, and Robot Odor.
Next week Looking Sullen,
which we'll combine with The Purposeful Lurch,
mastered in the first class.
Following that, Stealth Levitation and Telepathic Stammer.
Our remaining time we prepare for the exam.

There Is No Place That Does Not See You

You might change your life
based on dream dictionary
abandoned in Laundromat,
coloring book-size paperback
fished from utility sink,
splayed on folding table,
pages wavy as voice patterns
or antique window glass
but meanings plain
as air the equals sign
between all things,
then name your childhood
a long crawl on dirty floors,
lint-itchy, watching
a single red sock
fall the same among T-shirts,
playing jail with empty basket,
game show oohing
in steam and soap heat,
all the mothers, yours and others',
tapping ashes into cola cans,
one calling her children little
monsters, little bastards.

Next

Speaking of oxygen, it's everywhere, and thank heavens
all solids are visible, otherwise, abundant concussions.

Abracadabra, here to who-knows the walloping sunlight
over debris fields and detention centers, bordellos

and burglar bars as x-d jet streams quadrangle wide, any-
color sky, below which some number things drift,

newsprint unfurling in wind and car crash imminent
as birds in some flowering thicket flicker,

each driver about to say _____ or _____ on cell phone
at the intersection of _____ and Complete This Sentence.

Belongings

Thousands have drowned in the Rio Grande or adjacent canal,
part of a group whose numbers have become so large.
The deaths leave families to worry and wonder.

Some who die are never found. Silent, invisible deaths
surface in police reports like water from cattle troughs
fifteen days through harsh scrub.

A sudden storm sent a torrent of rainwater.
A two-year-old child survived by clinging to a ladder.
Dozens more people die of exposure.

Across the lonesome brush of South Texas,
a young man from Mexico or Central America
is an age at which death seems distant.

Crucifix. False teeth.
Matchbox. Recipe.
Deck of cards. Address.

When I Say Chair

I just mean chair, and not, for instance,
a rainy street in China
or meatloaf in the refrigerator
you should have thrown out weeks ago.

You can sit down like this
and relax, because it wouldn't be proper here
for a tulip to pass itself off as an ax handle
or a butcher's smock to pretend
it's anything like an eyelid.

Already you've picked up a book
and are turning the pages in a way
that doesn't in the least resemble
hummingbirds caught in the horse's throat
or someone falling off a building.

And now that the night has come on
like the night coming on, you put the book down
and look out the window:

the stars aren't made of iron
and starting to rust.
The stars aren't the dandruff
on a blind man's collar.

One Damned Thing After Another

Tonight let's dream of William Blake,
who said he saw his brother's ghost
ascend through ceiling, clapping
hands for joy, or how, so Napoleon's
soldiers might silently relay messages
past nightfall, not alerting enemies,
Braille began. My sleep's troubled
remembering X-ray anatomy of bat wings,
their unlikely, puppet-string bones
like lucky guess a child chalks
or ancestors carved in caves. We heard
them scurry through the dilapidated
mansion's walls. They cavorted
mornings, rose and swooped
while I laced my tie and tied my shoes.
I could have pulled the suicide
writer's ponytail but failed to,
sitting behind him in that huge room,
allegorical paintings depicting the new
world's conquest everywhere about us.
How often I'm bewildered by odd urges,
like longing at convenience store
to slip from holster the policeman's gun.
As the writer was praised for all he voiced,
I pantomimed to my friend beside me
threading my fingers through and tugging.
Somehow I believe and don't believe
this might have changed our lives.
When I think of Blake, I see him
plump and pink, cheeks almost plum,
eyes crinkled, Quaker on oatmeal. Neural
pathways grooved, I recall his wife
Catherine and him naked—Eve and Adam—
in their London garden. Recent thinking
says memory dwells diffusely, repeated
across cells and regions, so my ill will
lingers in many vicinities. Even altered,
no visions, only reckoning it 3-D
onomatopoeia, performative utterance
when I spray spittle when I say "Splash"

and fearing days for dollars, time left
equal to royalties owed, my dreams
peopled by people in stock photos.
Our daily store of sunlight replenishes
through church windows melting at glacial pace,
slower, lately, than glaciers. Google what
they were and did, gouging rivers and lakes.

Another Petition

Dear Doppler shift in soliloquy while plummeting,
Dear interpreted pattern of dispersing birds,
Dear sunlight scattershot on river ripples,
Dear phenomena simulacrum,
Dear background extras muttering "Rhubarb,"
Dear fingers through which money flits,
Dear firemen arrived in time to rescue cellar,
Dear vinyl's glitch, antique hiss and click,
Dear air, medium for all things,
Dear open and close parentheses the praying hands,
Dear weird feeling I think a landscape depicts when my slippery identity shifts,
Dear referent, whatever it *it* limns,
Dear someone, come here and tell me.

The Illusion of Autobiography

The recurrent first-person pronoun
emerges italicized in daylight,

blinking and tilting from tavern,
loiters in purloined doorway

recollection guesses Chinese restaurant
called *Chinese Restaurant*.

The fabled first-person pronoun,
indexical as any drifting *here*,

weaves now to now to now,
whatever endeavor, fleeing scene,

following hiss of dust mop,
dreaming on sleet-flecked bus

in dark everywhere eventual
tombstones weathers render illegible.

The ephemeral first-person pronoun
quivers like trestle or face hearing news,

dwells on memory of shoeprints in slush,
shivery cups of dusk. If I

am not my mind, who am I?
My urges? What happens?

Actionable

Scabrous, jackass Anstett slanders
non-stop, heckles the very air, badmouths,
bleeps the bleeping unprintable
expletive deleted what-all, blasphemes,

cowering, in "Ein jeder Engel ist schrecklich"
T-shirt, dreaming empty bottle
in ditch's hollow, frost across it astral,
fractal, cocoon inside it cloudy, fetal,

then uses these words in a sentence:
"Holy Ghost get-up again this year, all be-all
end-all, four-faced as Revelations, last chapter

tell-all, to get the good candy tossed in my sack,
then disappear with hair dyed off-brand
color: Rain-Wet Asphalt or Pigeon Flutter."

Infinitives

To divert you rainy afternoons,
grainy photographs of monster
footprints across lawns and roofs.

Terrible to love the sound of such words,
to think them floral:
mafioso, carcinoma, maquiladora.

To long to sing the sentence,
"Blending in in crepuscular raiment,
balaclava-clad assassins slink."

To tremble like aquarium skeleton
pirate sprawled across treasure chest on aqua gravel sea floor, bubbling
"Glug, glug, glug," blubbering "Yo, ho, ho."

To recollect childhood's homely totems, plastic cereal bowl pierced near brim
with stove-hot fork, wig on doorknob that terrified brother, lamenting hinge,
tar on tube socks where sun-melted asphalt splashed.

To skim the scum from boiling onions,
hunger to gnaw the moss from gravestones.

To yearn to blur—onstage, basement—drenched, shirtless, going ape shit on drum
    kit.

To scoop in cupped palms fizzing sea foam.

To make of life something
simpler yet ampler,
less the,
more or
and and.

To pine for faux hoax footprints to appear.

Or No

Maybe a mermaid feels fabled when the sailor sees her.
Maybe a mattress exists for the imagined and caresses.
Maybe a pillow's wrinkles are visible ripples of dreaming's wake.
Maybe spiders balloon their webs' threads, floating over floods.
Maybe a moon's to iron an ocean's creases.

Maybe luxuriance of sunlight on cell floor will save us.
Maybe we'll steal from port-town occult store means to summon demons.
Maybe market topiary seeds instructing shrubbery to grow those shapes.
Maybe contract outsourced labor to think these things.
Maybe found religion on belief that self is to swamp as soul is to liquid.

She Is Taking Off Her Shirt

She is taking off her shirt
like a short history of everything.

With the first button,
someone invents the wheel.

I can see her breasts now
as Socrates puts the cup to his lips,

and as she stops to touch a nipple,
Jesus is taking out a splinter.

By the time the night is over,
half of Europe will be burning.

Birthday

Cousins in a circle goad
the blindfolded one, spun

in circle and urged to burst
open with broomstick animal.

Piñata filled with birds' nests?
Piñata filled with spider webs?

Sticks? Crickets?
Forks? Scissors?

Piñata filled with wigs?
Photographs of accidents?

Piñata filled with darkness?
Piñata filled with silence?

Pig or donkey aunts and uncles
quarrel and what might spill

to earth in brunt of sunlight
and make the children scream.

Facts About Dreams

This dark the stars look eerie as X-rays
of animals, quadruped skeletons:
hippo, horse, elephant, camel.

Tender believing we're not alone, longing
for whatever one says the soul a quality
of light in autumn, sorcery of sunset on water.

In the vocabulary of interrogation, how define "industrial solvent"?
Exactly what we think?
Regardless, her eyes were aerial photographs.

Not sleeping, I orbit circumference of toothpick, matchstick,
cigarette, circle lunar surface, arctic blood
drop from which extends all matter.

Tomorrow, how magnify and brighten the grain of experience?
How not yank hair, beat chest, lope all fours, any field's beast?
Lit by fluorescents, why not snuff and bray among cubicles?

Close Shave

> *Why did God ask Abraham to sacrifice his twelve-year-old son?*
> *If he'd been thirteen, it wouldn't have been a sacrifice.*

Relief? regret? that we'll never read in native Danish
Fear and Trembling, contemplating weird vicinity
between universal and general as hammock straddles
span of land and air nor say one word to sway
distant objects, neither sloshing water over lip
of hotel bath nor tumbling tinned fish from shelves.
No continent sealing shanty leaks nor swerving bullets.
Cannot let attention stray again to nape of neck
in math class and fail to answer which more mass:
coins in cushions or planet's ants. Will not be restored
to old jobs: industrial laundry, pest trap factory.
Neither, dear Lord, hear nor heed your command.

Anything Helps

Imagine a haggard man imagines wild
animal seraphim floating over road kill,

remembers sunset colors of bodily
organs, conjures in road sign plywood

signs and wonders, scours off-ramp
grasses, all matter reducible to atoms.

I think he sleeps and dreams dreamed
script, *Sleeping in the Movies: The Movie*,

or sees years litter of thrill-colored
unmentionables out of which many step.

Maybe one's rarely so gladly mammal
as rain's first splatter on neck skin,

loosening grit. One states one's case
on cardboard, infiltrates an evening.

Maybe we'd rather yap in tavern,
contending: Who isn't trying

to forget something? The heart,
like any killer, has reasons.

Toward Ideal Table of Contents

Statues Bludgeoned by Sunlight
Phantom Apparatus
Headache Weather
Aspirin Slicker
Infinite Wishes
One More Sandwich
Soup for Ghosts
Coupon Trouble
Octopus Melee
Inventory of Lint
The Last Will and Testament of Uncle Clams Casino
Vermin Squirm
20,000 Leagues Under the Seep
Admiral Hijinks
Total Spittle
Laundromat Interlude
Listen, Citizens
Fiery Slump
Lily and the Swamp Glow Mysteries
Lacquer the Asteroids, Madam
Bargain Heebie-Jeebies
Ephemera Manor
Ply Wildly, Multinational Petrochemical Concerns! These Sea Creatures Will Not Grease Themselves!
Apocalysh
Ask the Twitchy Official

Camden

> *From the eyesight proceeds another eyesight...*
> —Whitman

Say we Google Earth then zoom and zoom until pixels blur and I confuse
outsized flecks for the infinite's distillate, with which our every cell's suffused.
Say I long to leave my brain to pseudoscience, yearn to marry the very air
as I hoped but failed to in his last residence on the unkempt block, car in flames
outside on asphalt, plywood board over door next door, men still sleeping
on stoops when I left, walking fast past the county jail. Dear Ineffable,
What brazen declarative about the world in general at last says it,
that on which the mind alights, momentarily placid and well-lit?

Thus This

Let the record reflect the witness
pointing to her own throat,
by facial expression imagining
how to sing about hive collapse
and convey a moment's creases.

With matchsticks and atlas
I charcoal anger's ranges
across pages like migratory patterns

and now abroad in the world
must run a distance equal
end-to-end to closed eyelids' pleats.

Let us plunge forth through summer's shimmer, winter's tinsel.

All year the dictator sleeps well, dreams again
he's a body of water, killing things and hiding them.

One story begins, "We never meant this to happen."
Another, "I never thought I'd tell this."

A Life to Say the Names of All the Dead

The Uncles, drunk,
funeral home parking lot,
fetch canned beer from car trunks,
walk two directions at once,
sway and curse and slur their slurs.

Every Christmas fistfights tumbling to frozen lawns,
squad lights on sheet ice.

The Uncles pass a flask, badmouth
one another, then you, and then your mother,
curse the God-damned
insert-your-plural-epithets-here
as a radio between stations screels
static's squelch and scribbles.

And the Grandfather's backyard junkyard,
axles, engines, corrugated Quonset, chain link
squalor snow exonerates
below curio like antique currency: rare, heirloom moon.

Any Shimmer

Matter in its disguises, dissolving at its rates,
one suspects there is this life no shape
some water, cloud or wave, each other's translation,
however briefly has not approximated.

Addressee, suspend in air wire armature
through which parabolas of dust motes rotate,
mimicking atoms' and planets' orbits,
approaching the shapes a mouth makes, singing.

Whence sprung my tragic sense and faith in goofy grandeur?
A constellation, though I trace much back to the invisible
hand of the market fingering my waistband.

Odd consolation, in the infinite continuum
mostly not existing as now I dread and generally fret
less the human condition than my peculiar one in particular.

Even uncertainty not what it seemed
conjuring time-lapse, stop-motion photographs—
Eadweard Muybridge's yawn, line of lips sprawled
as behind beard's smoke-color tumult
unseen strings of neck and jaw draw taut.

For my next impression, chronic exhaustion,
signature maneuver in elaborate,
prolonged ploy to become cadaver:
less a man than many renderings
of one flipped through fast.

What

Little so plush as all-at-once
all at once, totality its many places:
seafloors and rooftops, jails cells, galaxies,
mole on your clavicle to satellites circling earth,
my pocket's linty squalor and all the air in the Vatican.

Steady work, Lord, to make it look easy, the patina of authenticity.

Shame we cannot choreograph bee swarms
or clouds to form travelling lettering,
every language, spelling "Hello."

Portent

The fray of birds flickering over strip mall, for instance,
knotting and loosening in air brine of roofing tar
and next-door sea—vinegar, rain, rot—insists
something pressing to you and soon you insist,
memorizing, about rust-color sunset's special effects,
less pink-red dyed meat glistens than bit lip's red-pink
or red-red gone gutter leaves sepia of stabbed man's T-shirt.
You cannot prove he blundered past one morning
on footbridge over dribbling creek—throbbing traffic?—
and never breathed a word. The big fuss persists:
orange of flammable fabric, otherworldly orchid
scarlet in speckled patches beyond pay day loans,
pharmacy, discount cigarettes. As if slathered in lubricant,
each thing in teetering landscape gleams. Miracle, maybe
you think, body repeating. Lucky not endlessly.

Onlookers

Watching Ferris wheel unhinge
then roll through carnival,
outsized and awful,
a long way through midway
before final, rickety wobble,
like coin across bar floor
or hubcap after accident,
cries from other rides
and it a general blend,
some among us one supposes
thought—even then—thirst,
bills, disasters on television,
"rescind" an anagram of "cinders,"
"snow pea" of "weapons."
This did not happen. Much else did.

Prayer for Fervent Purpose

Whatever weather, wavy air, dripping,
snow sting, let me stand upright, forthright,

outdoors all day and night, traffic island,
churchyard, bare lot, repeating the umpteen

names of the principles that, standing up
for principles, standing there I stand for.

Mulishness, for instance, doing business
as Persistence, Laziness pretending

it's Conviction, me the 3-D rebus,
living emblem, allegorical statue

beset by phenomena, sweating or
frostbit, in outfit madman non-descript,

circled by birds whose cries I interpret
as urgent, clear calls of encouragement.

So-So, Also

Feeling forgiven, then forsaken,
feeling painted by Francis Bacon,
gauzy, raw, meat locker frozen.
Feeling ill-lit, feeling darkened.
Feeling hidden, feeling shrunken.
Feeling muddled, feeling forgotten.
Feeling the feelings that feel fallen.
Feeling hybrid of monkey, donkey.
Feeling pack animal down to least molecule.
Feeling floppy as seahorse on sawhorse.
Feeling looming disarray.
Feeling victim of mind-body struggle.
Feeling each morning the tired quarrel,
all fours along floors feeling my way.

Another Thing

Birds, that do not know their Latin names
or understand they're christened anything,

numbers swelling or dwindling,
skitter in wind, circle over auto impounds

and the open-early taverns
as my brain, that hothead, angers up,

then imagines a soul within the atom's width
between two fingerprints

or trapped in sawdust-clogged confines
of animal taxidermied to imitate its opposite:

face fierce, lips stretched, glass eyes looking wet.
What next? Win staring contest with memorial statue,

eyeballs marmoreal, in graveyard miraculous
with hailstones sudden from the heavens?

All reports the moon smells like fireworks.
I've come a long way to tell you this.

From *Moreover* (2016)

Thicket

Men outside the mission look biblical,
barefoot on sidewalks,
blankets for raiment.

Elsewhere that city an expert perfects
the crackle of liquor over ice in digital audio,
mist a sizzle and hiss.

Someone believes invisible threads
extend through all matter. Someone's haunted
by objects in pawnshops: power tools,

wedding rings, guns. Another wonders
with what is a body synonymous,
of what is a thicket indicative.

The Night There

In the night there are no guardian angels, but there is sleep.

Poor strategy combating insomnia
calculating hurdles a sleepwalking

Robert Desnos leaps around an oval.
Not "leaps" so much as swings one leg over,

straddles, then wiggles free from, slowly,
as if under water, jersey number less

number than punctuation mark or wiggling
scribble. As cinders crackle under slippers

he utters marvelous, improbable sentences,
eyelids maroon and hooded. Less "hooded"

than drooping as theater curtains or violet
cravat and smoking jacket I wish he wore

instead of striped pajamas in last known
photograph, Theresienstadt, 1945.

Fortune

Searching surgery mortality statistics
on phone in waiting room returns
Complete Concordance to Holy Scripture,
"I beheld, and, lo, there was no man,
and all the birds of the heavens were fled."
Thank whomever I will not return
to my old job baiting vermin traps,
hands damp in surgical gloves, thumbing
poisoned cubes of food all day into plastic
hollows then go home and drink beer
until I have to go and buy more. Workers
of the world, my brain knows better
but my heart's a communist, redistributing
wealth in perpetual revolution. No joke,
the specters. Hunger. Poverty.
Late-Era Capitalism, what next? Yes,
the long nineteenth century repressed
then killed everyone. Yes, all history
plague and conquest, tangle of skeletons,
every extremity of *What We'll Do for Money*.
Yes, life mostly tedium when not histrionic
as opera. For years I carried the fortune
in my wallet: *All of your troubles will soon
be over*. Pixels across the Internet portray
anatomy and famous people's babies.
Names create in the mouth and brain
the pucker and taste of things, fish, pepper,
onion, lemon, but do not, alas, replenish.
And now, thank whomever, among the 99%
surviving this procedure, you and your 1,200
thread-count laugh in the 900 thread-count air.

Geographic Cure

Say this for the universe: at least it's merciless
everywhere equally. Likely we're alone
in longing for clouds to collaborate with wind
and spell, elaborate, wavery script, *This Way
to the Grand As-Is,* then leak and spill where needed.
Land on fire, for instance, and where people thirst.
Number among my umpteen flaws detached glibness.
Who would disagree that little's glitchless?
I withdraw my petition for Arbortrary Day,
when I thought we'd rise in multitudes to fell
trees at random and appease the minor deities
who've not yet provided a passable answer
to the general question "Why?" Some say water
clairvoyant and render as evidence telepathy
of electrical current. Some assert a name not
worth the breath to say it. Some allege a raspberry
one seed's most direct and eloquent expression.

Parable

Multiply quantity of sunlight through windows
by total any Friday "At least it's Friday"

guffawed in offices.
How often I think you alive again.

Which will not happen.
Even if the latest celebrity tyrant commanded it.

Then my feelings feel burlap, texture and color.
Then I call on the fabled

shoulder angel and demon to help me,
but nothing. Not even a shimmering.

If it pleases the court
let me submit as Exhibit A my memory

of friend I last saw on earth
walking one block ahead in mid-size American city.

I did not hail and detain him. And then he turned.
Weather stringent, almost winter,

light paltry as frayed string, I recall sleet
in my ears and on my neck's skin, then eyes stinging

with tinge of chemicals from drycleaner's doorway,
smell not quite ammonia, not quite vinegar.

Moreover

We might graph weeks of life
waiting at red lights, days weeping
and sneezing, hours believing
little real, decades asleep and sleepy.
Good theory, we're all God's dream.

If only arcana marginalia penetralia
answered all. A "florid raggedness"
may describe the text or time.
Now I'm going to stand here
and tell you silence imagines itself

darkness in wooden desk, confined
to drawer with lingering scent
of pencils, dust, licorice. Insert
your face and whiff. Doesn't the grain
of air resist description, slippery grit?

Don't bones endure, numerous, named,
and the visible from distance stay
luminous and vague? These neighborhoods,
chain link and rubble, missile shells, bodies,
how to keep seeing? Smallest cathedral

that country that city an actual skeleton
ornaments the altar. An apple on black
plate decomposes, sheds its shape.
Hopeful, that the brain remains
lit all night like franchise on interstate.

Yes, No, Sure

Consider the notion of a thrown voice
traveling implausible distances, 12,450 miles,
for instance, half the circumference of earth,
from the ventriloquist's trachea, larynx,
pharynx, tongue, and lips to your ears, elongated

sound waves hovering like comic thought
balloons or miasmic veils over people, pastures,
promontories, water. Difficult to unhinge
from the present, then the future, wreck
toward which we slant. Oh, irrevocable if-then,

I want to believe an intelligence guides us
like I believed as a child Venus flytraps
eat lizards, small monkeys, birds. Like whatever
the ventriloquist said, approaching incrementally,
sunlight, none, are untouchable and anyone's.

Spell

> "Wring out the clothes! Wring in the dew!"
> —*Finnegans Wake*

Acquire vessel clear and clean as unobstructed air.
Erlenmeyer flask or whisked and scoured jar.
Into this, with eyedropper through blank page strain:

- Scintilla Ganges
- One dose Thames
- Iota Amazon
- One dash Seine
- Glimmer Volga
- Soupçon Yangtze
- Suspicion Yukon, Skagit, Mississippi
- Syllable Limpopo, Maputo, Sanaga

Outdoors, toss the water into any wind at hand.
Trace a ripple in the page's grit.
Smear each eyelid with a pinch of silt.

Limits

In my heart, that decaying neighborhood,
there stands a tavern, apt and shifting
name in neon: *Pour House*, of course.
Worse days, *Shots*. Everyone's drunken
uncles watch for hours waiting for horses,
Fat Chance, *No Such*, *Didn't Ask*,
to splatter silks across a sloppy track
or men to beat each other. Elsewhere,
flamingos and volcanoes, avalanches
and lovers' trembling breaths. Here,
through glass brick windows and burglar
bars, sunlight swells and fades across
increasing calendars, same and changing
faces, floorboards threadbare beneath the rail.

What You Mean by "I"

Maybe you've consumed so many substances
you're more chemical reaction than flesh,
more concept than substance and now must shush

your brain, that bossy loudmouth, with your brain,
but it's lizard, limbic, and won't be hushed.
Maybe I'm in barroom bathroom inhaling

capsules' contents from toilet tank ceramic,
off-white on off-white, while through sepia
tint of charcoaled liquor imagining more earth

under the earth, recent and vintage skeletons,
hidden rivers, tunneling mammals, umpteen
insects biding time. Who longs more for the exotic

promises of childhood comics: X-ray specs,
monster-size monsters, for God to collapse
the windstorms then fold them small as maps?

You who one morning oversaw windowsill's
miniature snow drifts, arctic past breakfast? Me
who traveled states and fell in love with the visible

skin between boot top and skirt hem ample at evening
bluegrass concert in Austin, Texas, sunset palpable?
Who's most dumbstruck anything exists?

Subject

Which simpler: Smuggling
surveillance schematics
through time zones as tattoos
under eyelids, calculating
word count—just verbs—
over cell phones one hour
one city, Mumbai, maybe,
or counting beds across
the continents in which
laborers sleep in shifts?
Please explain your answer.

Surgery channels on basic cable
show glistening innards but not
restricted skin, so many dots per inch.
Are you for or against?

Perhaps we grant the actual
too much credit. Now
write the steps between tree
and ember, portrait, ash.

Thinglish the universe speaks
through objects in syntactical,
rebus-like relation. Suppose
a sentence of gutter debris says
all matter resided in space
smaller than a match head.
Arrange an infinite number of items
to keep it from doing so again.

Landscape with Disclaimers

Dear Antipodal Who-Are-You, Polar Coeval,
Maybe you're anachronistic hypochondriac
beset with longing for antique maladies:
Barber's Itch, The Vapors. Maybe you're proof-
reading pamphlets, eyes weakening each word,
maybe envisioning pigment in petrified insect,
color of its final prehistoric meal—bird's blood?
grass sap?—intact. To reach you, oh, palindrome:
crust, mantle, outer core, inner core, and so on
backwards. Magical thinking, thinking
you physically opposite thus antithesis.
When bubbles cycloned clockwise one noon
in my refilled beer glass while live on television
my government invaded compounds, what
did you feel? Were you also like me drafting
catalog description for imaginary painting,
Landscape with Disclaimers, "For this blank space
picture grasses in which several winds contend"?
Is that how you squander days, so-and-so I'm lonely for?

Apparently

While my government authorized attacks
and across the planet more people than fathomable
suffered in ancient and latest ways,
I documented software procedures, repeatedly
mistyping "appears." In ordinary strip malls
somebody's children navigated drones over distant villages
with keystrokes and joysticks as I touched your legs and neck.
Sea levels rose and species disappeared.
I wondered what I would say to calm the panicked
young man who thought before he died
he wanted to get drunk first eight- or nine-thousand times.
I knew many hurt and did little.
I worried I'd stay no better than the worst I'd been.

The People

Say it plainly: the country breaks
my heart, its heartlessness, the ragged
all day in libraries, our suffering
industrial complex, killer drifting
motel to motel, mother in kitchen,
coffee cup of vodka, pills on counter,
blur and sheen on look of things.

All winter fields and poems
fill with snow, almost audibly.
Snow settles and sifts. In blanks
between buildings, shadows darken
drifts. Pointing to distance circled by birds,
"Over farther yonder" hollers father.

Children pelt each other as corporations
measure viewers' eyeballs' flick and jitter,
the better to sell so much during programming.
Where mice exist, they represent the stubborn,
burrowing inscriptions. Landscapes stun,
and vistas: the word *created,* the word *equal.*

There Arose a Smoke

Sooner in photographs of lens flare
discern strangers' faces and wager
dollars on their guessed names as walk
a distance to oust the powers. See
photographs of extinct animals as elegies
for swarms and herds, the collective
nouns they were named. While we slept
dew assembled, then steamed free
of leaves and grasses. Perhaps you
should call your journal of one-word
poems and stories *Squander*. Insofar
as our brains seem bundles of protocols
to render the immaterial physical, the physical
immaterial, we're constrained to hemispheres.
Suppose the body has inhabitants. Who claims
it facile to declare it vessel? Say the sun's
remorseless. Squint and blot it with a thumb.

Believe

Fear last thoughts, whatever deathbed,
hospital cotton, heating grate cardboard,
plunging to asphalt in increments,
I jinx eternal existence,
one theory, with final synaptic flickers
sitcom spinoff theme song,
household cleaner jingle,
carnival organ-flecked doggerel
I loved at 15, crooned by arrogant brooder,
or racist quips of ex-coworkers and in-laws,
or growing ill on ill-advised
carnival ride, The Catastrophe,
machinery loud as crack of iceberg calving.

Judge of everything awful I've done,
jail only the id, which did it,
that made my body its robot
in service of lizard brain, limbic,
and let me hear hiss of sheet on skin,
her voice saying my name
or latest favorite faux expletive,
"Musket fumbler, musket fumbler, musket fumbler."

Selfie Stick

My chief occupation: occupying space.
Distinguishing feature: possessing mass.

In the dream of me I dream me
taller, younger, smarter, kinder. Maybe

I 3-D print a 3-D printer to 3-D print
myself a mirror. What happens

in and outside its promiscuous surface?
Everything, gradually. Austere,

what's whittled, but let's carouse
in miscellany: drums, cantatas, graffiti

every color, vernacular names of flowers,
"Rocket Larkspur," "Five Spot," "Mexican

Hat," lovely as James Schuyler beginning poem
"Hooray." Glorious, considering our history:

minuscule, pursued by animals.
My manuscript called *Afterlife Memoir*,

bound for big box store stacks, starts:
I died and went to heaven and it terrified

and bored, like work and war, like life
itself, which I'd just left, which looked

from that wide respite like waves
in paintings, as paradise did, like seeing

energy slowed. I longed then to be beset
with irritants, rust from chains across suit

pants or in my squint the sting and scald
of sleet, then found myself now here again.

Ipse Dixit

May as well wager
which word prettiest—
reciprocal? meadow?
discrepancy? surgery?
accelerant? imbroglio?

plumage? hush?—or
dispute fabric pattern
best paired with mood—
houndstooth sorrow,
paisley whimsy—as argue

up there, where prayers
contend and birds skirt
the many invisibilities, open
source in uncopyrightable
sky, through scrambled

chatter of unfathomable
disaster and celebrity
scandal the unknowns
that worry over and love us
and which the greater pity:

that we want or what we want.
Call at your convenience
to say again how wet
earth smells where you live.
Describe its fumes and spices.

Noble Truths

"To exist is to suffer, the Buddha and I say,"
I said like a jackass to the woman

beside me in the mostly empty tavern
lit like a cafeteria middle of the day.

Pale ovals on the bar top showed
where hands rubbed paint away,

lowering and lifting glasses repeatedly
as we did all afternoon, suffering hits

of the 70s our bartender played,
". . .rocks and stones and birds and things. . .,"

". . .a man selling ice cream. . .." I thought
then said, "There is no end to my desire

to never hear these songs again."
"You talk like a jackass," she said.

To the Office for the Inevitable's Futile Redress

Sirs: Thank heavens all we see is surface:
shirt front and not breathing lungs
or heart squeezing blood, faces'
expressions, not muscles' striations.
Am I the only one who fears my thoughts
are eavesdropped on, any meeting
imagining attendees naked and/or
punching each other? Weird, huh?
Me? I like best dusk, when hills look cut
from cardboard, colors synonymous. Prayer?
Praise vigilant windows, all day and night
see-through. Praise that small sea, a spoon of soup.

Natural

Pigeons fat as prelates
in antique paintings

strut and peck
cement for scraps.

Their raiment gleams
shabby, Salvation

Army colors, gutter
water and gasoline.

Shaped like cursive
capitals, Dutch shoes,

they roost at intervals
on lines and roofs.

My brother and I
my mother says mimicked

in cribs their warbles and coos.
They people every city,

rise from sidewalks,
stutter over skylines

to their own applause.
Last winter a crow

and seagull quarreled
over bread at dawn

as a rabble of pigeons
and I looked on.

The Historical Record

Somewhere no more
exact than "Europe"
she says words
from burned books
flutter, hover
in clouds like gnats,
ashy, illegible.

The crackle underfoot
in City of Splinters:
fragments of houses,
taverns, churches.

The man you meet shivering
in vestibule, assure him
even mountains move
through time, here from antiquity,

and every language has a name
for weeping if not for when
our insides feel weather-swept.

You Say You'd Be at Sea at Sea So Stay Away, Land's Stowaway

> *Position is where you*
> *put it...*
> —Robert Creeley

What had been here interrupting air
who knows. Sky's a big tent and little lasts,
not stars or clouds or their images on open
water and irises. God it seems is sworn to silence.

Who doesn't love a loudmouth narrator blurting
wild claims, "Everything's in history like a building
in flames" or "The invisible's filigreed from time,
that material first too ample, then too scarce"?

What had been here interrupting air? Something
like eyeballs or animals or cells mid-division,
planets or atoms or planets' fragments in orbit.
Are those ovals in the ovals pupils, nipples, mouths?

Which creatures are these swarms of, ideas'
outlines, what continents, oceans, estuaries
in this lavish of speckles eye-blue, sunlight,
leaf-green, fish roe, blood stain, earth?

Can it soothe to imagine what had been
one's life a series of points, some
number planes, so many frames, memory
abstracted to geometry, time to outline,

like reckoning rainfall methodical, pinpoints
on purpose, different tints at varying distances,
then lying on sidewalk or dirt in sprinkling
or downpour and looking its source in the face?

The Bargain

"Tempus fugit, motherfucker" yells
our after-dinner speaker to late arrivals

at conference I dream, "Ducking and Slugging:
Writing Realistic Fight Scenes."

Then suddenly my dream
career is proofreading footnotes

for *Proceedings of the International
Congress for Ennui.*

One lengthy passage
reveals the message,

"In lieu of pleasant childhood
recollections please accept this

photograph of vintage rainfall
the dead move through, unspeakably sooty."

All Things

Now change these lines based on market demand.

Now dwell on language's poverty in light of every moment's amplitude.

Now think how keen any sensation, with which no expression is commensurate.

Now recollect sad startle of gunshots at sunset that neighborhood where we drank on the roof drugstore tequila and discussed the crisis of the authorial "I," its limits and ranges.

Now believe narrative a kind of noise-cancelling device.

Now tap sternum with four fingers five times to ensure continued corporality.

Now imagine gown sewn on nine ghosts, simple yet haunting.

Between A and The

Among the squandering for which we'll one day also have to answer,
searching cathedrals and passages for a luminous answer.

Clouds' shadows sprawl and fall
and fail to act as empty field's answer.

The first telephone number you knew?
Dial it now and no one answers.

How to tell the children death
runs in the family I cannot answer.

For relatives' deaths, "heart attack,
car wreck, shellfish" ought to be their answers.

Call the mortuary John Doe
any name, he will not answer.

We may as well demand The Ineffable
once and for all provide an answer.

Under oath, transgressor Anstett
refuses to please render a simple yes-or-no answer.

A Valediction

If only naming moods would change one's.
If only saying dollar amounts replenished accounts.
What thoughts I thought, sad about the failure of these poems
not to nourish or swerve bullets but to please me and editors better.

Likely only in my mind prehistoric-looking catfish ply
steel tubs the color of thunder through Asian
grocery plate glass that block in Illinois
between donut shop and tattoo parlor.

In some mood we'll claim the mind
yearns to all phenomenon ascribe
correlative status, turn each object to allegorical statue,
the world not only not meaningless but too full of purpose.

Sometimes all that stills a panic:
imagining cartoon monsters mating
or opening specialty concept restaurant
in which we're maltreated with food

or hearing John Donne drawled to steel pedal
and musical saw, high-and-lonesome
screech and squall, eerie caterwaul,
"Batter my heart" and all.

Certainty

A man rises from a conference table,
tired of acronyms and everyone
saying them, weary of phrases like
"A lot downstream hinges on this…"
and "We're productizing cloud offerings."
He walks through door after door
after door to the parking lot, whispering
names of countries and capitals,
then continents and body parts and colors.
From the asphalt he lifts what he guesses
a pigeon's feather, oily, iridescent,
and thumbs its filaments, conjuring
the restless winds that fluttered them.

A Legacy

Likely we'll never nunchuck our way out of trouble
in drug lord's warehouse on steamy, far-flung
capital's outskirts, Asia, maybe, or South America,
then flee through brazen pluck and stunning wheelwork,

never successfully command animals to stop eating
each other for one second, broker peace between species,
and collaborate, constructing world's tallest serial creature
that quells the evil in all men's hearts, never even e-mail

the mayors of cities whose names strike us funny
and organize tours: Buttermilk, Bloom, Protection,
Acres, Greasy, Ulysses, Zigzag, Eek, Accident, Kismet.
Good days recall the texture of a child's knees in summer,

crazy quilt of scabs. *Parents! Recount your dreams
to your children* the surreal postcard implores.
Just before dawn we barely see the edges of things.
They look wispy, pencil-sketched, shimmering and frail.

Big Statement

Then the air looks wavy
like it's full of umlauts.
Then the landscape looks iffy
and the people in it

like molecules shimmying.
Then the video all things
stream buffers. Then reality
suffers packet loss and jitter.

Sublimating self
in service of the spectacle,
we undermine powers
arranging phrases, no?

Then the moment's fresh
prospects blossom
like flowers of fruit
transformed to flesh.

Then we're in history
like a robbery in progress.
Then we're in the world
like a building in flames.

Plots

I tell my children the central premises
of 70s television: a man and his son
run a junkyard, people's dreams
come true on a secret island, two cousins
race hot rods and the law. They snort,
"You're kidding." I have not recounted
the story of Job nor the childhood
of Moses. Some think film deteriorated
after the earliest, purely documentary
shorts: Fred Ott, with comically drooping
mustache, inhaling snuff and sneezing,
or workers, mostly women in long aprons
and bustles, leaving the Lumière factory,
walking with purpose, released to the evening.
I describe again the shambling homicide
detective in trench coat, one-eyed and cunning.

Best Intentions

How say clearly, without frippery,
we sorrow and wallow? It burns
energy imagining everything breathing
some day dead: elephant, prisoner,
hummingbird, senator. On earth
still let's hand-craft small-batch respites.
All we wanted was to make sounds
keen. Forgive us, Lord, our shopping
malls, weapons, cities people people
only in memory. And you, me in past,
so morning-after dew looks sticky
and sunlight vicious, remember nobody
unsquanders days. No spells rescue,
even one hundred thousand times writing
"I will not plagiarize," wrist and fingers
sore, then numb. Think of details dark
obscures as drinkers' pupils widen
in tavern murk. I see the future and say
there's weirder weather no matter sky
blue as window cleaner or paint named
"Sky Blue." Are we the physical form
anger assumes? As a nation we struggle
with television series' ambiguous endings.
Should we extrapolate from the evidence,
playground flagpole's shadow glacial
all day, that everything's artifact?

A Tragic Sense of Life

While the latest outrages unfolded
and flared, as atrocities blossomed,

we clicked around and watched
first a cat synchronized to dance music

slinking along piano keys, then middle-aged
threesome in ill-lit room, discount motel

you said from bedspread's vivid
floral pattern and geometric wallpaper

against which shadows blurred and stuttered,
soundtrack televised newscast, accents

hard to place. The women looked plain, man
pale and flabby, physique and bald spot

approximating mine. Then you turned
from the screen to see weather happening

out the window. Who put us in charge
of watching dirt clods rain dissolves,

those particular cracks in earth obscured
by generalizing mud? All the news

in the world and I skim online comments.
Probably we're slight oscillations

detected nowhere in the universe.
Probably we hardly know how to feel.

Emblem

Midway through the night
he woke feeling like so many
pounds of commodity pork
bellies or corn meal then brain
like split wood and legs
batteries leaking less him
than things with prices
and uses who wouldn't rather
be reading Dante or hearing
diligent rain then birds
stirring in skinny trees

He does not know which
to have tattooed half-inch
serif script across back
Energy is Eternal Delight
or *the eye altering alters all*

To transport himself he thinks
he'll think about the child
who slapped the glass of van
Gogh's *The Starry Night* actual
on MOMA wall or beaches
scantily clad in kelp and shells
and stars bare and water plain

Imagining the bright and tiny
fire razored in already
he sweats and feels
neck skin prickle
and rib nerves pinch

Last time obscuring
a name above the heart
above the heart he flinched
and said it had been years
*It all comes back quick
don't it* the artist grinned

Moreover

Now I name my punishing
moves for antique hymns,
"Just a Closer Walk with Thee,"

name my darkest fears
for household objects,
"Lightbulb," "Spoon."

A wind travels vastnesses
out of the past, from the day
we started in fits and starts.

Once I believed my miseries
luminous and original.
I honed my little sorrows.

Oh, in the sweet by and by,
may we praise whatever is
stubborn and nimble in the spirit.

❋

As if in scrap of air inches
before my eyeballs words
saying answers appeared

out of order, street signs
rearranged to fool invaders
is how it feels when I kiss you,

my body magnetized,
little on earth
as it might be but I love you.

❋

Do we long again to stay
up late recounting scars'
etymologies, lousy

jobs, arguing yes
or no a God
as across the planet

sunlight picks out
landscapes' brightwork,
scenarios from which

we're mostly absent,
and then the birds
commence their racket?

✺

I hew to this skeleton
to all others' exclusion,
believe nothing

will hurt me,
wind the wide-shouldered,
skinny-fingered,

malingering over empty fields.
People of the future,
I renounce the future!

✺

Probably in distant bed someone
dreams about you or 6,000
venomous spiders spilling from walls.

In whose official version
do clouds mirrored in flooded meadow
insinuate labia and wings of demons?

What's imagined at the last?
Flames and frantic animals?
Parents who left you here on the planet?

✺

And you, with your angers, passions, saddest
memory you tell no one,
who in the sky's echelons

wills air wherewithal, cure-all
then selects for each of us sacred manuscript,
patchwork of scraps of text from world's birds' nests?

Halloween Costumes: Reclusive Creator or End of All Being

You, whose sleep I imagine
so like my own, have you never woken
supposing excruciations in far-flung places?
Are you not like me contemplating
objects and forces and their possible orbits?

Who needs to know now more terrible truths this late in history?

Why not then long to loll on sunset-tinged
grasses in barbiturated dusk, blades lit
one side, shadowed other, verso, recto,
as wispy fringes on earth's edge
dwindle, pink and purple?

Who doesn't long to feel hopeful against all evidence this late in history?

Some mornings I want to lie
to everyone, say "It will all be fine"
to the children, surly before school,
and implore neighbor who scowls and stares
when I nod, "Let us glory in the hinge each moment is."

Why is there something rather than nothing this late in history?

My new plan: lengthen poems 40%
by larding in every few words names of plants
and flowers but first must learn to discern difference.
Then say what stage of bloom and decay. Then describe
birds' flight in weather's shifts and list the animals' habitats.

How the months, years, millennia that dawdled whip along this late in history.

Class Struggle

Billionaire, I'd order in compound
hot dog stand where they treat me
rudely to keep me humble.

I like best to dine in establishments
with racks of free magazines
advertising pre-owned vehicles,

appliances, and weapons
near gumball, temporary tattoo,
and religious icon machines.

Places where plates are paper
food came wrapped in and air
smells good: salt, frying fat, onions.

Maybe I'll earn the money
with daredevil stage antics
or canvases I paint and scrape,

creating expansive masterpieces
of presence and absence
then spend my free time broadcasting

from birthing centers descriptions
of newest humans with effusive
discernment of wine reviews:

This yowling infant, classically
wrinkly, exudes outrage, whiff
of bewilderment, notes of piss.

Always Go To Other People's Funerals, Otherwise They Won't Come To Yours

You can observe a lot by just watching.
The future ain't what it used to be.
It's like déjà vu all over again.
I never said most of the things I said.

The future ain't what it used to be.
No one goes there nowadays, it's too crowded.
I never said most of the things I said.
When you come to a fork in the road, take it.

No one goes there nowadays, it's too crowded.
A nickel ain't worth a dime anymore.
When you come to a fork in the road, take it.
It gets late early out here.

A nickel ain't worth a dime anymore.
You can observe a lot by just watching.
It gets late early out here.
It's like déjà vu all over again.

Lines Written in the Anthropocene

Enduring experience intermittently, suddenly
we're inside distant planet, navigating the heart of a star.
While little occurs, a narrative develops.
The construction of self looms despite the post-human.

We're inside distant planet, navigating the heart of a star,
using fingerprints for sextants and eyelids' insides for maps.
The construction of self looms despite the post-human
enigma of controlling machinery and being controlled.

Using fingerprints for sextants and eyelids' insides for maps,
already time dissolves our problems to granules.
Enigma of controlling machinery and being controlled,
names of asylums and prisons evolve to synonyms.

Already time dissolves our problems to granules.
I would like to take a stranger's face between my palms and apologize.
Names of asylums and prisons evolve to synonyms.
I would like to take a stranger's face with me everywhere I go.

In Search of Lost Time

Think of the stream that thaws and freezes,
stoplights bouncing and swaying on lines,
whales keening, their hearts large as cars.

With forklift and hand jacks, No Way
and I unloaded pallets of boxes,
wire parts from overseas ready for coating.

In the street past the bay door, clouds
of exhaust wobbled sludge-slow,
tinting darker old snow.

Later, over our heads in the tavern, toy
horses pulled beer wagons for hours in ovals.

Memorial Plaques

Crossing the intersection, Pine and Liberty, she feared
it all meant nothing. This house, he felt the saddest ever.
Here I first kissed you, and that bench, quiet for once,
we imagined scrutinizing glasses of water for ice skates'
inscriptions. Let statue of general on horseback stand
for mood one afternoon, furious the world outlives us.
There, where no patrons remember when, a fist-size
meteor surprised through ceiling. That avenue, drunks
teeter in doorways dusk to dawn to dusk to dawn.

From *Please State the Nature of Your Emergency* (2017)

Final Animal

Translucent amphibian or molecular
invertebrate, scavenging rodent

or stubborn ungulate, whatever
it is endures all manner of onslaught

for that imaginable unimaginable
forthcoming moment it's the last thing

blinking and breathing in landscape
covered with almost comical

numbers of corpses, largely us, no
one living to analyze prayer as a form

of fluid dynamics or correlate lightning
to astral anomalies, no one remembering

the famed island let alone its tavern
where painters slugged each other

and how much a beer and shot cost,
no recalling terraced squatters' shacks

of South America or the fact
ancient Egyptians believed frogs

emerged from flooding
and the coupling of land and water.

Against All Evidence

Because we cannot believe in God
the Monster entirely but believe in God
the Monster a little, we'll never be elected.

We own these souls. Won't someone
fix them, uncover and preserve forever
patches of sidewalk sun to sit in?

In this game we walk
our characters forward
and have no control over
what rushes toward us.

Caravaggio painted these faces
in 1607 and 1608 and 1610 respectively
then disappeared into history. How pretty
his features in concealed self-portraits.

Maybe I'll vote my subconscious this year,
Walking Scissors for mayor, *I-Don't-Want-
To-Kiss-a-Man-Yes-I-Do* for senator.

I must tell you my guess about God.

If the flooding continues, the lions, who swim,
could cross the moat and climb the walls.

Next Election

Maybe inject chlorophyll beneath skin to grow own food as we go.

Maybe clutch in each palm handfuls of fat as hedge against vanishing animals.

Maybe class up cursing with smattering of Latin.

Maybe drive to supermarket stunned by afternoon sun faint like photocopy of photocopy of photocopy of smudge, see-through against sky window-cleaner blue.

Maybe tell nice officer who asks we're operating under influence of symbolic aura, pale and vivid colors and dot-to-dot constellations we daylight take on faith.

Maybe hope at last our suffering possesses the symmetry of Dante.

Maybe lie on courthouse sidewalk reciting petition drafted first by inscribing in bartop whiskey puddle the symbol for infinity.

Maybe recall crows wheeling in sunset over dollar store.

Maybe move lips while reading novel whose plot points magic and spells resolve.

Maybe remember Melville wrote *Moby-Dick* in western Massachusetts near whale-shaped hill.

Maybe imagine mansplaining the ways of God to man.

Maybe compose libretto for opera buffa celebrating domestic life, *La Dolce Rigmarole*.

Maybe make claims drastic and hyperbolic: neutrinos inoculate flesh against spontaneous combustion, one example, and each instance comes at us at the same velocity: suddenly.

Things We Say

After latest tragedy, let's drift
asleep listing words for what
fish, oblivious in waters, do:
Plunge, glide, dive, sway.

Our daily allowance of banalities
includes again that strange phrase,
"realistic fiction."

Among many nevers:
Billionaire or seeing
through spider's ocelli.

As sidewalk sleeper dreams
of icy vodka careening
in bloodstream's arena,

as sea assails the shore
with shells, kelp, itself,

think of labor horses
perform in lyric
and actual, foam of lather
slicking necks.

Oh, bury me
like battle reenactor,
musket in casket.

Before then, let's,
you know, *it*,
on historical attraction.

Let's volunteer hours
overseeing elections.
This candidate believes everyone
deserves what happens.

I Came Here Looking for Something

On shadowed path before sudden, lumbering bear,
play dead or perform world's greatest trembling

aspen impression. Alive again in tent or cabin, sip
thimbles or saucepans of whiskey until moonlight

glints on all the pitchfork points inside you. Admit
that little's louder than God's silence. One day, full

of coffee and sorrow, maybe playing Buck Owens'
"Streets of Bakersfield" on repeat while reading fusty,

meticulous history of prosody, you'll say for their sounds
"behemoth," "jacaranda." Who wouldn't go back to be born

in hospital named for cigarette brand or despot or become
insect drifting like hammock napper, ferried in dent of wind?

Autumn Morning in Philadelphia

I choose to believe the evidence
of a world before or after I'm in it
hoax and fake as some have claimed
dinosaur bones and fossils, salted
across the earth by God to test our faith.

Yet all over this city mothers serenade babies
in many languages and in the courtyard
around Independence Hall chestnut and elm
leaves fall in patterns never the exact same again,
large as the parchment of historical documents.

A Gap Where Things and People Once Had Been

This museum object label called by curators "tombstone" fails
to list dust and color-dulling sun among the artists' materials.
We hazarded a guess at price at auction but grew distracted
estimating gallons per second evaporating in Amazon basin.
Maybe we'll redefine light years calculating square inches
of skin darkened then lit so many days then dividing by all eternity.
Will it help or hurt believing air a kind of flab we wallow through?
Fleeing suffering, we flee everything, water tainted with prescription
and illicit drugs, shadows cast across asphalt by eolian litter divining
how we'll die, merlot and pineapple sunset, wood grain's and wood
smoke's ripples, waves with grit in them. Likely we'll never hear
the ruffle and flutter of paparazzi shutters, us the apertures' objects,
gate number something or other, LAX or PEK or elsewhere. In distance
of earliest existence, our origins' elements linger: river and brick, stream
and stick, two strangers' bright idea. Fine print stipulates rain one day
pinpoints us, x-y coordinates toward which so much descends.

The Beginnings of Sorrows

In my country, number one
    for billionaires, prisoners, franchises
offer menu consistency. What lies
    dormant today in the collective
unconscious? Akin to tintype, sun prints
    itself on structures and skin.
As we age our vocabularies
    expand, contract with names of maladies,
despots, lands next for neglect.
    Never so many in history displaced
and in transit, our weather's breaking
    records again. In maps, see crimson,
scarlet, ruby, ochre, folly, wine,
    rust auguring sea level rise
and agricultural loss. Whom,
    in interminable funeral, transcend
time's passing imagining nude?
    How hope some ideal elsewhere,
mirroring correspondence, spooky
    action at a distance, perfects
all motion? In my country,
    stick's best trick: stay stuck
years marking spot sprung culprit
    returns to at long last as salmon
and tangerine sunset tints the earth.

Last Will

What will the children say if I say I fear
our fates are decided in secret meetings
and my best advice remains ignore
many things, maniacal yowling and floating

casino's calliope? Bequest? Avoid these accidents:
Committee chair or huddled under trestle,
wondering which hinge reddest, rustiest,
most sunset among world's abandoned

amusement parks, every continent, machinery
grease long ago evaporated. An animal urge
overwhelms to confirm the taste of dust and blood
then wince hearing screech and squeak. Insert

description. Append assertion. Let imagination drift
and memory steer. Remember your mother, shape
of her face yelling and yawning, looking
blank, pretending not to hear a solitary word.

Insert Here Lengthy Disclaimer

Daylight in cinder block tavern a drunk
man said he killed his friend in accident
on accident driving into tree and went to corrections.

After umpteenth drink he said this
as the jukebox played the sad, slow songs
you imagine and on the television potential
contestants jumped around hopeful in costumes.

There's a hole in the bucket. With what will I fix it?

Nobody there cares if you're thirsty.
Nobody cares if you've eaten.

A man-shaped cloud of mayflies appears
to operate tilt-a-whirl in Iowa river
town murky summer evening in memory.

Answers vary by region, how many
syllables in "fire" and "wheel." Nothing
of our substance remains as-is, but orbits

of atoms and particles persist, those circuits,
as microscopic and monstrous animals
navigate volumes of water. All matter

serves as units of measure: universe,
whisker, planet, satellite, tooth, box springs
and mattresses burning along avenues, stacks
of axles and tires fenced by train tracks.

Dear Arresting Officer, No joke:
How do we endure?

I ordered another, pledging allegiance
to my regular, The Never Enough.

Essential Dilemma

Man the only animal
argues yes/no animal

and which the body's
essential dilemma, each

bit its expiration, strung
with nerves, fraught in general,

says, too, praise the intricate,
difficult work of blood vessels,

galaxies, atoms. Praise
ancestors struggled up

from forlorn saltwater.
Praise all matter

rubbed between fingerprints
eventually granules.

❉

Loitering at intersection,
teetering as wind

confettis grit—eyes,
ears, lips—feeling nervous

system like flowering umbrella,
how in so much eavesdrop

accurately and glean
from speaker's blurry

features which: *Museum
on fire* or *Museum of fire*?

❉

Filmed slow-motion in daylight, opulence of disaster.
Night: time-lapse tracery, stars' and headlights' longhand.

Being of Sound

> *I've got these arms and legs that flipflop, flipflop!*
> —Pere Ubu, "Navvy"

Goodbye alpine meadows, goodbye
the ultimate in live nude extravaganzas.
Goodbye moonlight on burglar's crowbar,
goodbye sunlight on rusty screen door.
Goodbye numbers and all their variants.
Goodbye critters, goodbye varmints.
Goodbye water. Goodbye land.
Goodbye foggy notions, and lucky
guesses, I'll miss you most.
Goodbye rain and goodbye roofs.
Goodbye glint and goodbye glare.
Goodbye noon. Goodbye false dawn.
Goodbye officers and goodbye miscreants.

I've said the ugliest and prettiest
things I felt and felt no better
after, either, something in me ill
at ease, quivery, living.

All my life I labor to stymie
the body's ouster of the so-called soul.

Count me among occupants of alleys in which such ilk eke,
among burned books in which the exact word lurked.

While able I'll
inhale chemical,
forestall nightfall,
wrestle jackal,
Australian crawl waterfall,
wriggle ankle,
curtail rainfall,
whistle madrigal,
puzzle know-it-all,
banana peel automobile,
eyeball fireball,
kindle rubble,
unveil pinhole,

PLEASE STATE THE NATURE OF YOUR EMERGENCY

unspool molecule,
overrule minuscule,
distill vitriol,
overhaul the overall,
crank call all you-all.

Please State the Nature of Your Emergency

Whatever suffering we have coming,
some among us deduce huge, unseen
planets from objects' warped orbits.

On the many channels, no answer.

Imagine each dawn and dusk
the aftermath of some god's
vast wrist flick,

then think of all the streets
and blame the light
for making visible litter
of leaves and paper wrappers.

Graves await their claimants,
but please do not construe
the beautiful, open air as invitation.

Consider all the air the lungs
must share and sort,
the water blood becomes,

the tired surprise
of anyone's death
a kind of sunrise.

History happens while we clean
clothes and dishes, worn
from many labors.

But you were talking
about the phenomena
of snow and thunder,
fresh patch interrupted
by succinct blood drop.

Across mountains fog
renders other,
ellipses of birds flicker.

Angry, I forget exist
beaches feet score,

PLEASE STATE THE NATURE OF YOUR EMERGENCY

lines strung between windows
from which clothes drip
water to a street

and stack of red bricks
around lamppost on corner
near car equal to annual pay.

How quickly life can change.

Facts Are Stumping Things

In government by stunt
recall the verb to eat like animals
flesh from which we're estranged
then remember we're meat that makes
us strange and wonder which of many
its is one *its* referent: whole people or insect
on arm slapped somewhere in sepia.

While evils are sufferable, ask a gullible uncle
to circle in documents names of our enemies.

Then select the range of years
from which to read daily a paper
and pretend now's then.

Then maybe go *en masse* to that thin
sliver, Togo, then solo north to Burkina Faso.

Nothing Funny

> *It takes the corrupt, ectoplasmic shape of a prayer*
> *Or money, that connects with a government somewhere.*
> —Edwin Denby, "The Shoulder"

What to quip about the president's
budget moving wealth from poor to rich
as in the waiting areas cable channel
news crawls name the places latest
troubled loner shooters surface
between pharmaceutical commercials?

One headline: "Thanks to crushing
medical debt, crowdfunding sites boom."

Better to imagine all the waters
composing snow or argue
plant and animal cells more
action than location, less
substance than function.

A neighbor has posted a photograph:
Shelves and orderly jars of soil,
each labeled with name of victim,
glass housing silt and twigs.

The Tomorrow We Stumble Into

In aimless and meaningless universe, our existence
improbably occurs, given statistics.

Circling the earth glide myriad instruments
diagnosing conditions from numerous distances.

Long last, after so very much of it,
we remember the lessons of history:

>   a. Levels of damage: Bad, Worse, Horrific.
>   b. Never invade Russia in winter.

With some number number 2 pencils let's draft petitions
against waste and abuse in graphite and timber industries

then squander years steeping selves in moon-landing conspiracies
and cataloging sorrow, frivolity, and death-metal taxonomies.

Museum of Invisible Scripture, pamphlets hand-written in vinegar
react to heat, then words appear, urgent, the color of tea.

Oh,

each object hurt
les to a future, ur
ges into its ow
n vanishing.

That eventual then, when
the brain's the iddest
ever, thoughts scurry
like emergency
services personnel, no?

I like my prayers make-do, homely,
fashioned from the at-hand.

To quell all fugitive feelings,
I watch footage of the rich
indulging in luxury products
then dream of the cryptozoological as if
the sight of them might slow diseases.

Leaves flicker to their shadows
past statue in courtyard,
general of battle whose cause
no one living recalls.

Remember the painting in Italy, St. Jerome
clapping and weeping over his doll-like Jesus?

In the office, behold:
light rays splintered
by thin tip of thumb tack.

If only my work all day
were contemplating the voluminous
output of Anonymous.

I feel great love and pity for people
plural, though one by one they irk.

Who from bridge to river
falls so many Mississippis?

Now let's tell
the saddest stories.
You start.

(An open parenthetical ends the poem

Index of Poems by Title

$500,000 Policy, 83
93% of Statistics Wither Under Scrutiny, 31

A Gap Where Things and People Once Had Been, 227
A Legacy, 205
A Life to Say the Names of All the Dead, 167
A Possible Reprieve, 38
A Tragic Sense of Life, 209
A Valediction, 203
Actionable, 156
Afterlife, 67
Against All Evidence, 222
Against Interpretation of Dreams, 143
Alas It Is So, But Thus It Must Be, 25
Alias, 79
All at Once, 132
All Things, 201
Always Go To Other People's Funerals, Otherwise They Won't Come To Yours, 215
Ample Evidence, 139
And Then, 78
Andre the Giant Has a Posse, 19
Another Petition, 154
Another Thing, 174
Answer, 99
Any Shimmer, 168
Anything Helps, 163
Apparatus, 17
Apparently, 189
Appetite, 122
Ardor, 98
Are Those Real Songs or Did You Write Them?, 136
Atoms in Their Orbits, 129
Autumn Morning in Philadelphia, 226

Bare Lot, 59
Being of Sound, 232
Believe, 192
Belongings, 150
Best Intentions, 208

Between A and The, 202
Big Statement, 206
Birthday, 160
Blessings, 113
Bluff as a Theorem, 133
Blur, 55
Bullseye, 10
Burglars, 117

Camden, 165
Can't Get There from Here, 27
Care and Feeding, 146
Certainty, 204
Class Struggle, 214
Claw, 37
Cleaning, 82
Close Shave, 162
Coliseum, 134
Costly Repairs, 29
Country, 106
Cusp, 46

Declarative, 92
Drinks, 69

Each Day, 123
Emblem, 210
Errors and Omissions, 131
Essential Dilemma, 231
Evenings Full of Forfeiture, 52

Facts About Dreams, 161
Facts Are Stumping Things, 236
Final Animal, 221
Five Definitions, 54
Flight, 116
For All the World, 8
Fortune, 179
Free Beer Tomorrow, 124

Geographic Cure, 180

Glass Mingled with Fire, 118
God's Job, 74
Good Morning, 73
Grammar, 77
Gulf Coast, 88

Halloween Costumes: Reclusive Creator or End of All Being, 213
He Do the Polysemy in Different Voices, 28
Heaven, 40
History, 68
Holes in the Story, 93
Hoopskirt Parish, 51
How to Remove a Fishhook, 5

I Came Here Looking for Something, 225
If I Had Another Face, 76
If/Then, 7
Immutable, 15
In Search of Lost Time, 217
Indeed I Was, 121
Infinitives, 157
Insert Here Lengthy Disclaimer, 230
Ipse Dixit, 194

Just to Change the Subject for a Second, 32

Labor, 57
Landscape with Disclaimers, 188
Last Will, 229
Lay My Burden Down, 89
Lessons, 44
Life and Death at the DMV, 90
Limits, 185
Lines Written in the Anthropocene, 216
Lorem Ipsum Flotsam Jetsam Harum Scarum Punctum Dictum Cockalorum, 20

Man Saves Own Life, 36
Manos 84.13.72, 135
Matter, 75
Measure of Revenge, 48
Memorial, 145

Memorial Plaques, 218
Menace, 47
Mercy, 64
Mission, 14
Mississippi Delta Blues Musician's Picture Altered on Commemorative Stamp Presents More
 Positive Image, 60
Moreover, 182, 211
My Sentimental Education, 81

Narrative Impulse, 138
Natural, 197
Needling, 110
Next, 149
Noble Truths, 195
Nothing Funny, 237

Oh,, 239
One Damned Thing After Another, 152
Onlookers, 171
Open Beer Stores, Running Buses, Marigolds Small Miracles on Police Station Lawns, 56
Or No, 158
Other Words, 6

Parable, 181
Pharmacy, 35
Physics, 49
Plea, 12
Please State the Nature of Your Emergency, 234
Plots, 207
Portent, 170
Possible Report Made in Error, 11
Prayer Against Dying on Camera, 96
Prayer for Fervent Purpose, 172
Prayer for Recompense, 112
Prayer for Safe Travel, 97
Progress, 147
Proposal, 3
Proposition, 114

Redolence, 105
Reinventing the Wheel, 108

Satellites, 94
Self-Portrait as Jackass on Dash Cam, 130
Self-Portrait in Corporate Offices, 109
Self-Portrait with Product Placement, 141
Self-Portrait with Spoiler Alerts, 140
Selfie Stick, 193
Shanty, 80
She Is Taking Off Her Shirt, 159
Shift, 58
Simple, 115
Slow Learners, 41
Small Favors, 50
So-So, Also, 173
Some Clarifications, 16
Some Final Statements, 30
Somewhere the Patch of Dirt Awaits, 13
Spell, 184
Storefronts, 107
Subject, 187
Sustenance, 53

Tabernacle, 119
Tell Me, 63
That Feeling of Impending Doom? Impending Doom., 137
The 99 Names of My Band, 22
The Barber, 42
The Bargain, 200
The Beginnings of Sorrows, 228
The Historical Record, 198
The Illusion of Autobiography, 155
The Night There, 178
The People, 190
The Sonnet Again Enjoys a Moment, 26
The Ticket Taker Speaks, 45
The Tomorrow We Stumble Into, 238
There Arose a Smoke, 191
There Is No Place That Does Not See You, 148
Thicket, 177
Things We Say, 224
This Street, Any Street, 43
Thus This, 166

To the Office for the Inevitable's Futile Redress, 196
Toward Ideal Table of Contents, 164
Trouble, 103

Undressed, 104
Unresolved Conflict, 142

Vast Gist, 18

We All Have It Coming, 9
Wet Floor, 39
What, 169
What Profits a Man, 84
What They Want the Poem to Do, 4
What You Mean by "I", 186
When I Say Chair, 151
Why Skylines, 62
Winter, 95
Work, 91
Worry, 61

Yes, No, Sure, 183
You Say You'd Be at Sea at Sea So Stay Away, Land's Stowaway, 199

Photo by Lesley Ginsberg

Aaron Anstett has received the Nebraska Book Award, the Backwaters Press Prize, and the Balcones Poetry Prize, among other honors, and has served as a regional poet laureate, instituting a continuing project that places the work of local writers in waiting areas. He works as a technical writer and editor and lives in Colorado with his wife, Lesley.

www.ingramcontent.com/pod-product-compliance
Lightning Source LLC
Chambersburg PA
CBHW032126160426
43197CB00008B/531